IMAGES
of America

BALTIMORE
RADIO AND TELEVISION

Completed in 1959 by a construction crew of just 12, the Television Hill Candelabra Tower was a joint project of the city's three existing TV stations—WMAR, WJZ, and WBAL. Originally 730 feet tall, a 1964 addition brought the tower's height to 997 feet. (Courtesy John Ziemann.)

ON THE COVER: As Professor Kool, the only thing Stu Kerr taught was fun. Each week, he would lead the school song, sung to the tune of "Jingle Bells." "We like school, we like school, cause it's lots of fun. Singing, laughing, playing games, blues are on the run. We like school, we like school, love to hear the bell. For our teacher Professor Kool, let's give him a great big yell—ahhhhhhh." (Courtesy John Ziemann.)

IMAGES
of America

BALTIMORE
RADIO AND TELEVISION

Gary Helton
Foreword by Ed Graham

ARCADIA
PUBLISHING

Published by Arcadia Publishing
Charleston, South Carolina

Printed in the United States of America

Library of Congress Control Number: 2019930635

For all general information, please contact Arcadia Publishing:
Telephone 843-853-2070
Fax 843-853-0044
E-mail sales@arcadiapublishing.com
For customer service and orders:
Toll-Free 1-888-313-2665

Visit us on the Internet at www.arcadiapublishing.com

This book is dedicated to all the men and women, past and present, who instilled in me a love of broadcasting. Thank you.

CONTENTS

FOREWORD

Radio is my life—no, it really is. My earliest memories are usually tied to radio. On my sixth birthday in 1943, I was eating breakfast and Jim and Phil Crist were having fun on WFBR. One of them said, "Happy birthday, little Eddie. If you look behind your sofa you'll find something nice." That was traumatic. Stunned, I realized that radio was real. Most people old enough to remember radio of the 1940s also remember that radio was the only free source of entertainment, information, and connection to the world. TV didn't exist. Radio featured programs like *Inner Sanctum*, *Your Hit Parade*, and *Bing Crosby*—live entertainment. When news broke, it was on the radio in minutes, or you could see it on a newsreel two weeks later. All of that changed in the 1950s when TV came along and became the new source for entertainment and information. That's where this book really begins. Radio took on a new mission. It became intimate; it was your companion in the car and your connection to the person on the air was quite different from listening to a scripted drama. The personality became a friend of yours, bringing you great music. But it was also a one-on-one relationship that was unlike any medium before. I loved working in radio for 45 years in Baltimore, Washington, New York, and Seoul, Korea. People always ask me questions like, "Who was that guy who played a trumpet on the morning show?" Hard to remember the hundreds of on-air personalities, even some people I worked with over the years. Gary Helton (who eats, sleeps, and lives radio) is bringing us a photographic look at the people who made Baltimore radio unique and wonderful. It's a treat to see pictures of Baltimore radio talent. This book will jog your memory and bring back thoughts and feelings from the real Golden Age of radio—and TV. Baltimore was a special town of neighborhoods. George Carlin said, "It's eight o'clock in Los Angeles! It's nine o'clock in Denver! It's ten o'clock in Chicago. In Baltimore, it's 6:42! Time for the *Eleven O'Clock News*." People from Baltimore understand.

—Ed Graham

ACKNOWLEDGMENTS

I want to express my sincere appreciation to everyone who provided information, photographs and ephemera for this book. Thanks to Brian Belanger, curator, Ellen Dahl, museum assistant, and the board members at the National Capital Radio & Television Museum for their time, labor, and generosity. Thanks also to Tom Conroy, George Felton, Jay Guyther, Marian Wolfe Shuman, Fran Minakowski of Maryland Public Television, Mary McManus Guba, John Baldwin and Sharon McNicholas of WBAL-TV, Paul Bicknell, Bob Bell, Gary Michaels, Don Lehnhoff, and Siobhan Hagan of the Mid-Atlantic Regional Moving Image Archive (MARMIA) for their submissions, and to the late Royal Parker. My gratitude to Ed Graham for writing the Foreword and helping me identify some of the people in these photographs—you still owe me lunch. To my son, Jason Helton, thank you for bailing me out of some computer difficulties—as usual. And finally, special thanks to John Ziemann, a man who literally dug WMAR's history out of the dumpsters and preserved so much of it. Thank you, Z, for your time and labor getting everything out of (and putting it all back in) storage, for sharing your knowledge and your stories, but most of all, for letting me try on Professor Kool's mortarboard. Great big gobs of greasy grimey gopher guts to you, my friend.

INTRODUCTION

Radio—and later television—brought entertainment and information into homes and businesses for the first time. Prior to that, there were the usual books, magazines, newspapers, perhaps a piano, and Edison's phonograph. But for the most part, if you wanted to be entertained in pre-1920s America, it required a trip to the neighborhood movie, vaudeville or burlesque theater, a local church, park, or concert hall.

Baltimore was a bit behind the developmental curve that would become "broadcasting." Pittsburgh's KDKA had signed on November 2, 1920. But it would take another year before Calman Zamoiski's "wireless telephone" station designated "3RM" could be heard, broadcasting from his home at 2527 Madison Avenue. Four months later, on March 26, 1922, Zamoiski received a license to operate from the US Department of Commerce which, prior to the creation of the Federal Radio Commission—now the Federal Communications Commission (FCC)—oversaw the new industry. Baltimore's first radio station took the call letters WKC, operating from the top floor of the family's business, The Joseph M. Zamoiski Company, at 19 North Liberty Street.

A total of 74 days later, on June 8, 1922, WEAR was heard for the first time. Musical performances and an address by then mayor William F. Broening were featured that first day. Owned by the *Baltimore American* newspaper, the station would become WFBR two years later. That same year, 1924, saw Zamoiski's WKC cease operation. By then, however, WCAO was operating, with WCBM joining them in May 1924. Finally, WBAL came on the air on November 2, 1925. For the next 16 years, these four stations delivered all the music, news, sports, local, and network programming listeners could consume.

The period from 1925 to 1941 was fairly stable. Announcers and programs came and went, but for the most part the four stations, while competitive, maintained a peaceful coexistence, and an ever-increasing listenership. Many network radio stars rode their popularity into the movies—something that would later be duplicated with television. Bob Hope, Red Skelton, Jack Benny, Bing Crosby, Abbott and Costello, and others enjoyed cultlike status across the nation. Meanwhile, local stations continued to produce programs and air talent—as announcers would be called—that, in terms of popularity, rivaled the networks on a smaller scale.

Arthur Godfrey had served as a radio operator in the US Navy between 1920 and 1924. In 1927, Godfrey was attending specialized radio training with the Coast Guard at Curtis Bay. Two years later, he made his way downtown to WFBR, where he sang and played ukulele on a local talent show. The experience led to a regular, albeit brief, weekly program, before Godfrey would be spirited away to Washington and NBC-owned WRC.

Baltimore-born Thomas Garrison Morfit III had dropped out of school to pursue a career in radio. He worked briefly as an unpaid host on WFBR, but was lured away within a few weeks by a paying offer from WBAL in 1937. National attention quickly followed as Morfit became first the announcer for, then cohost of a program called *Club Matinee*, on the NBC Blue Network. During this period, he became Garry Moore, a name chosen by a listener in Pittsburgh as part of a nationwide contest.

On March 1, 1941, WITH became Baltimore's fifth radio station. Meanwhile, the development of television continued. Baltimore was America's seventh-largest city then and a key player in the country's defense industry. As such, the city was an important and impressive destination for aspiring broadcasters, even if their stay was only brief. Kenneth Williams Fertig Jr. was one. Born in Canada, Fertig adopted the professional name of Kenny Williams in the 1940s. After spending time at WFBR, he went on to announce and act on network radio and television, and may be best remembered for his work on the TV game shows *Video Village* and *The Hollywood Squares*.

Another was Eugene Rubessa, who honed his skills at WITH before heading to New York's WNEW. Later, he became Steve Allen's announcer for the original *Tonight Show*. Professionally, Eugene Rubessa was Gene Rayburn, the genial host of *The Match Game*, network television's highest-rated daytime show during the 1970s.

In 1947, television arrived, with WMAR premiering on October 27. It was owned by the *Sunpapers*. Their competitor was the Hearst Corporation, then publisher of both the *Baltimore News-Post* and the *Baltimore American*. Hearst also had its sights set on television, but WMAR beat them to the punch by five months. Initially, WMAR had no offices, studios, or employees with TV experience. Based at the Sun Building, an ornate structure that once occupied an entire block of Charles Street between Fayette, Redwood, and Hanover Streets, WMAR first broadcast only from remote locations using mobile units. A 26-year-old *Sun* reporter named James Kenneth McManus was tapped to be the first face and voice on Baltimore television. Within two years, he was hosting his own network variety show for CBS. Then in 1961, McManus, now known as Jim McKay, began a long association with ABC when he became the host of its new weekly anthology program *ABC's Wide World of Sports*.

For the next 20 years, Baltimore radio and television stations increased in number, exposure, and influence. In 1946, WITH became the first to occupy the FM band. Others followed, including WCAO in 1947, WMAR in 1948, and WBJC in 1951. But FM signals left much to be desired. Using the VHF part of the radio spectrum, these sound waves, while static-free, could not travel past the visual horizon and were obstructed by hills, mountains, and tall buildings. Jack Wells was the first FM radio announcer in Maryland, working an eight-hour shift—very long, by radio standards—on WITH-FM. As technology improved, more FM stations came on line, including WFDS (later WBAL, then WIYY) in 1958, WCBM-FM (now WWMX), and WAQE (WLIF), both in 1960.

Meanwhile, Baltmore's AM stations were flourishing. News, popular music, network programs, sports, witty personalities, and all manner of unique local shows dominated. WBMD and WSID both debuted in 1947, followed in 1951 by WWIN. WAYE set up shop in Dundalk in 1955. That same year, WTOW began broadcasting from Towson. Finally, in 1961, WISZ became the last local AM station, with studios and transmitter in Glen Burnie.

On TV, WBAL (11) and WAAM (13) joined WMAR (2) in 1948. Baltimore's fourth station, WMET (24), did not come along until 1967, followed in 1969 by WMPB (67), which in those days was called "educational" TV. Then, WBFF (45) signed on in April 1971 and, finally, WNUV (54) in 1982. The original Channel 24, WMET, operated out of the old Avalon Theatre on Park Heights Avenue. Under powered, the station was limited to transmitting in black and white only. That, and its microscopic budget, caused the station to go dark in 1972.

What follows is a sampler, so to speak—highlights of the first 75 or so years of broadcasting in Baltimore. It is my sincere hope that any exclusion not be interpreted as an intentional slight. There are just too many people and programs to include in this limited space.

—Gary Helton
January 8, 2019

One

STATIONS

Between 1921 and 1941, Baltimore's first six radio stations were created: WKC, WEAR, WCAO, WBAL, WCBM, and WITH. Of these, WKC ceased to operate in 1924, and WEAR became WFBR when the station was sold to the Maryland Guard's 5th Regiment. From this foundation, additional stations were established from the late 1940s to 1961. As a result of this expansion, and because of ownership and format changes, call letters frequently changed. From those humble beginnings, there are now more than 30 radio and television stations licensed to Baltimore or an adjacent suburb. WCAO is the oldest in continuous operation using its original calls, followed by WBAL. And while WCBM debuted in 1924, it went off the air briefly—the industry term is "silent"—due to a bankruptcy filing in 1987. WFBR, sold twice in the 1980s to out-of-town concerns, briefly became WLIF-AM in 1990, and then WJFK-AM. Today, it is WJZ-AM. The last of the so-called "heritage" stations, WITH-AM, is today WRBS-AM. The Hearst Corporation is the longest-tenured station owner in the market, having purchased WBAL-AM in 1935, ten years after it was established by the Consolidated Gas Electric Light & Power Company of Baltimore. Over the years, Baltimore AM, FM, and TV stations have been represented by a veritable "alphabet soup" of call letters—everything from WAAM to WZFT. One frequency, 104.3 FM, has had 10 sets of calls since its inception in 1946. Originally, WITH-FM, it became WDJQ in 1974, WITH-FM (again) in 1978, WBSB in 1980, WVRT in 1993, WSSF then WOCT in 1994, WFXB in 2002, WSMJ in 2003, and WCHH in 2008. It adopted the WZFT call letters in 2009. While on local television, Channel 13 came into existence as WAAM, switching to WJZ in 1957 when it was purchased by Westinghouse. And Channel 24, which began as WMET, evolved into WKJL, WHSW, and then WUTB. Today, with all the selections offered by WiFi and cable, it may be hard for some to imagine a time when only 2, 11, and 13, and a dozen or so radio stations existed.

This austere studio belonged to WFBR when the station was located on St. Paul Street. Signing on as WEAR in 1922, the station was initially owned by the *Baltimore American* newspaper. Sold to the Maryland National Guard's 5th Regiment, the call letters were changed to represent "World's First Broadcasting Regiment." (Courtesy National Capital Radio & Television Museum.)

WCAO's offices, studios and transmitter were located at 1102 North Charles Street, and later the Upton Mansion, an 1838 Greek Revival country house located at 811 West Lanvale Street. Visitors were greeted by an overlay on the floor declaring the station "the Voice of Baltimore." (Courtesy National Capital Radio & Television Museum.)

In 1924, WCBM's first home was the Chateau Hotel, at the corner of North Avenue and Charles Street. Reportedly, the station's calls were derived from "Chateau, Baltimore Maryland." In later years, WCBM was based here, in the Sears Community Building, near the intersection of North Avenue and Broadway, situated within the parking lot of a Sears retail store. (Courtesy National Capital Radio & Television Museum.)

After it was sold to the Maryland National Guard, WFBR began broadcasting from the 5th Regiment Armory, constructed in 1901 and site of the 1912 Democratic National Convention. This 1920s image features signs promoting the station's sponsors and encourages visitors to participate in a broadcast of *The Inquiring Reporter*, with Henry Hickman. (Courtesy National Capital Radio & Television Museum.)

Little is known about the broadcast that was taking place in this 1920s photograph, except that it occurred at WCAO or WEAR. (Courtesy National Capital Radio & Television Museum.)

News was an important component of local radio, and WFBR boasted the first mobile unit for remote event coverage. Seen here in Mt. Vernon around 1930, the vehicle was equipped with its own control room. (Courtesy National Capital Radio & Television Museum.)

BALTIMORE BROADCASTING STUDIOS WBAL

FREDERICK R. HUBER, Director

ADVANCE PROGRAMS

·· FOR ··

WEEK of MARCH 3rd, 1929

[EDITOR'S NOTE.—These schedules are arranged with earliest date at the bottom for the convenience of daily papers in clipping. Publications reprinting the programs in a group should reverse the order of dates.]

WBAL
BALTIMORE
Eastern Standard Time—1060 K. C.—283 Meters—10 K. W.

SATURDAY, MARCH 9th, 1929

6.30 to 7.45 P. M.—WBAL Dinner Music
7.45 to 8.00 P. M.—"A Week of the World's Business," reviewed by Dr. Julius Klein (NBC)
8.00 to 8.30 P. M.—Pure Oil Program, featuring the Goldman Band (NBC)
8.30 to 9.00 P. M.—Interwoven Entertainers (NBC)
9.00 to 9.30 P. M.—Pan-Americana (NBC)
9.30 to 10.00 P. M.—WBAL Ensemble—Soloists: John Wilbourn, tenor, and Nathan Cohen, xylophonist
10.00 to 11.00 P. M.—The Marylanders—John Lederer, conductor Soloist: Elmer F. Bernhardt, baritone
11.00 to 12.00 P. M.—Slumber Music (NBC)

WBAL
BALTIMORE
Eastern Standard Time—1060 K. C.—283 Meters—10 K. W.

FRIDAY, MARCH 8th, 1929

10.30 to 11.00 A. M.—The Choristers, with Marimba Band (NBC)
11.00 to 12.00 M. —RCA Educational Program (NBC)
3.00 to 3.15 P. M.—Philip Crist, tenor
3.15 to 3.30 P. M.—"The Interpretation of Contract Law for the Layman," by Judge Charles W. Heuisler, Dean of the University of Baltimore
3.30 to 3.45 P. M.—Edna Burhenn, soprano
3.45 to 4.00 P. M.—Short Story Dramatization, by Elise Lee Cohen
4.00 to 5.00 P. M.—Pacific Little Symphony (NBC)
6.00 to 6.15 P. M.—WBAL Sandman Circle "Strange Adventures in Far Places," told by Lady Baltimore
6.15 to 6.30 P. M.—Luden's Male Quartet
6.30 to 7.00 P. M.—Penn-O-Lene Pageant
7.00 to 7.30 P. M.—Esskay Hour
7.30 to 8.00 P. M.—Dixies Circus (NBC)
8.00 to 8.30 P. M.—Musical Art Gallery
8.30 to 9.00 P. M.—Armstrong Quakers (NBC)
9.00 to 9.30 P. M.—Wrigley Revue (NBC)
9.30 to 10.00 P. M.—Philco Hour (NBC)
10.00 to 10.30 P. M.—Hudson-Essex Challengers (NBC)
10.30 to 11.00 P. M.—Musical Memories

WBAL
BALTIMORE
Eastern Standard Time—1060 K. C.—283 Meters—10 K. W.

THURSDAY, MARCH 7th, 1929

3.00 to 3.15 P. M.—Walter N. Linthicum, baritone
3.15 to 3.30 P. M.—"Problems of Transportation," by Raymond S. Tompkins, Assistant to the President of the United Railways, Baltimore
3.30 to 3.45 P. M.—Margaret Jones, pianist
3.45 to 4.00 P. M.—"The Easter Bride Selects Her Trousseau," presented by Hutzler Brothers Company, Baltimore
4.00 to 5.00 P. M.—Salon Music by "The Calvertons"
6.00 to 7.00 P. M.—Parks & Hull Dinner Hour
7.00 to 8.00 P. M.—WBAL Wind Ensemble—Felice Iula, conductor

WBAL
BALTIMORE
Eastern Standard Time—1060 K. C.—283 Meters—10 K. W.

TUESDAY, MARCH 5th, 1929

3.00 to 3.15 P. M.—The Vernon Trio, comprising Emory Rosa, pianist, Walter de Lillo, violinist, and Howard Mitchell, cellist
3.15 to 3.30 P. M.—"Modern American Poets," by Elise Lee Cohen
3.30 to 3.45 P. M.—Sol Sax, pianist
3.45 to 4.00 P. M.—"Food for the Vegetarian," by Anna Trentham, Director of the Bureau of Home Economics, Consolidated Gas Electric Light & Power Company, Baltimore
4.00 to 5.00 P. M.—Salon Music by "The Calvertons"
6.00 to 6.15 P. M.—WBAL Sandman Circle "Stories You Can Play," told by Lady Baltimore
6.15 to 6.30 P. M.—Luden's Male Quartet
6.30 to 7.00 P. M.—Stieff Cameo Concert
7.00 to 8.00 P. M.—Amoco Motorists
8.00 to 8.30 P. M.—Stromberg-Carlson Program (NBC)
8.30 to 9.00 P. M.—Michelin Men (NBC)
9.00 to 9.30 P. M.—Three-in-One Theatre (NBC)
9.30 to 10.00 P. M.—Dutch Masters Minstrels (NBC)
10.00 to 10.30 P. M.—Lew White, organist (NBC)
10.30 to 11.00 P. M.—Freshman Orchestradians (NBC)

WBAL
BALTIMORE
Eastern Standard Time—1060 K. C.—283 Meters—10 K. W.

MONDAY, MARCH 4th, 1929

11.00 A. M.—Inaugural Ceremonies (NBC)
3.00 to 3.15 P. M.—George Bolek, pianist
3.15 to 3.30 P. M.—Book Review, by Dr. Edward L. Israel
3.30 to 3.45 P. M.—Viola Hewitt, soprano
3.45 to 4.00 P. M.—"Obstruction of the Food and Air Passages," by Dr. W. F. Zinn, of the Medical and Chirurgical Society, Baltimore
4.00 to 5.00 P. M.—Salon Music by "The Calvertons"
6.00 to 7.00 P. M.—Cloverdale Dinner Hour
7.00 to 7.30 P. M.—South Sea Islanders (NBC)
7.30 to 8.30 P. M.—Roxy Program (NBC)
8.30 to 9.00 P. M.—Automatic Duo Disc Program (NBC)
9.00 to 9.30 P. M.—Edison Hour (NBC)
9.30 to 10.00 P. M.—Real Folks (NBC)
10.00 to 11.00 P. M.—The Pattersons

From the week of March 3, 1929, this WBAL program schedule included offerings such as the *Esskay Hour*, *Food For The Vegetarian*, and tenor Philip Crist, who would later host WFBR's *Morning in Maryland*. WBAL was heard at 1060 KC at that time. (Courtesy National Capital Radio & Television Museum.)

WCAO moved to the Upton Mansion from Charles Street in 1927. The staff gathered at the entrance for this c. 1940 photograph. The white-haired man behind the WCAO microphone is Lewis M. Milbourne, president of Monumental Radio Company. Longtime announcer Charles Purcell can be seen over Milbourne's left shoulder. The women in the back are Mary Lewis (left), a secretary, and Mary Lamb, the switchboard operator. The remainder are unidentified. (Courtesy National Capital Radio & Television Museum.)

WBAL was first owned by the Consolidated Gas, Electric Light & Power Company, forerunner to Baltimore Gas & Electric, and was based at the utility's headquarters in the Lexington Building on St. Paul Street. Later, operations moved to 2610 North Charles Street. In this undated photograph, Galen Fromme (standing) and Tom White (seated) are checking reports from the various wire services. Teletype machines made quite the racket. As a result, many stations dedicated a special room for them. (Courtesy National Capital Radio & Television Museum.)

When it signed on in November 1948, Channel 13 was WAAM-TV. Still in its original building on Malden Avenue, the station's call letters became WJZ when it was purchased by the Westinghouse Broadcasting Company in 1957. (Courtesy MARMIA.)

In the early days of WFBR, the transmitter and tower were located in the east Baltimore neighborhood of Orangeville. After a storm damaged the tower, everything was relocated to Waterview Avenue, along the Middle Branch of the Patapsco River. (Courtesy National Capital Radio & Television Museum.)

Channel 2's very first broadcasts were done from the field using remote equipment, until the first studio and offices could be set up in the Mathieson Building, currently known as the Bank of America Building on Light Street. Shortly afterward, space was created for the station within the Baltimore Sunpapers Building, about a block to the west. (Courtesy John Ziemann.)

WFBR used this early studio, in their St. Paul Street location, for vocalists and musical programs. Note the use of curtains, wall panels, and area rugs for acoustical purposes. So many facets of the early days of broadcasting were created on the fly. (Courtesy National Capital Radio & Television Museum.)

He was still a skinny kid from Hoboken but was on his way to becoming a heartthrob in this undated photograph. The best was yet to come for Frank Sinatra, seen here visiting the Upton Mansion and WCAO. His female admirers, believed to be station employees, are unidentified. (Courtesy National Capital Radio & Television Museum.)

The building that housed the Centre Theatre, as well as WFBR's Art Deco studios and offices, was constructed in 1913 and originally served as an auto dealership and garage. Situated on East North Avenue at Lovegrove Street, the station's entrance would eventually be in the rear, on Twentieth Street. (Courtesy National Capital Radio & Television Museum.)

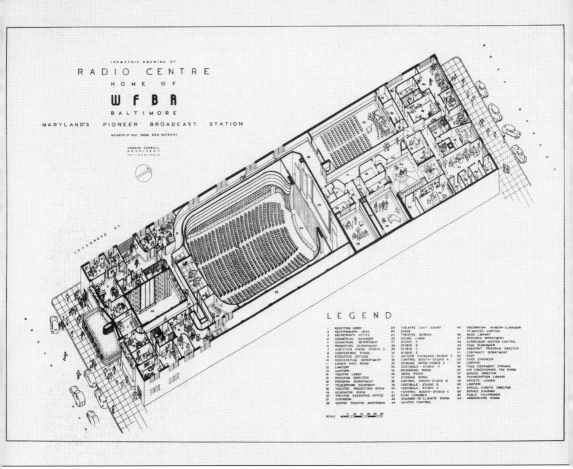

Philadelphia architect Armand Carroll designed the Centre Theatre and WFBR complex, dubbed "Radio Centre" in the late 1930s. It featured an Art Deco design, multiple studios, offices, and an expansive reception area. The building was actually owned by local businessman Morris A. Mechanic, who would later be a driving force on the city's performing arts scene. (Courtesy National Capital Radio & Television Museum.)

WFBR's spacious and well-appointed lobby featured a reception area, with an early aerial view of the Inner Harbor—then referred to as "the Basin"—about 20 blocks to the south. Studio A was the largest performance space, big enough to accommodate a large audience. (Courtesy National Capital Radio & Television Museum.)

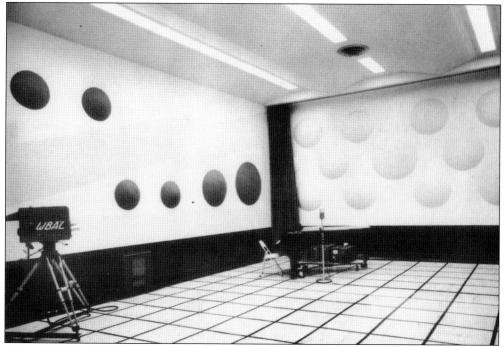

Before WBAL radio and television built their spacious facility on Television Hill, offices and studios were located at 2610 North Charles Street, a six-story building near Johns Hopkins University. WCBM moved in when WBAL left. Today, it is an indoor storage facility. (Courtesy National Capital Radio & Television Museum.)

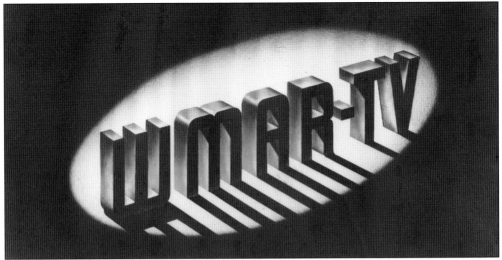

This simple image represents Baltimore television's first station identification graphic. Broadcasts on WMAR-TV began October 27, 1947. The first voice heard was that of *Sun* writer Jim McManus—later known as Jim McKay. (Courtesy John Ziemann.)

News and public affairs were a staple of early radio broadcasts. WFBR's mobile unit gave it an advantage over other stations. This image, from 1929, shows Pres. Herbert Hoover at the WFBR microphone, speaking to a crowd gathered in front of Baltimore's city hall. (Courtesy National Capital Radio & Television Museum.)

WMAR's mobile units have a special place in American history. When Pres. John F. Kennedy was assassinated on November 22, 1963, CBS had no mobile units available to cover the funeral in Washington. All had been sent to do NFL football games. WMAR equipment and personnel filled in admirably. (Courtesy John Ziemann.)

POWER - 250 WATTS KILOCYCLES 1270 Operating Full Time Telephone, PLAZA 6030	**W–F–B–R** Owned and operated by **Baltimore Radio Show, Inc.** 7 ST. PAUL STREET -:- BALTIMORE, MD.	Rates Effective September 1st, 1930 STUDIOS: 8th FLOOR CHESAPEAKE BANK BUILDING 7 St. Paul Street Telephone, PLAZA 6030

DAY—7 A. M. to 7 P. M. 1 Hour - $60.00 1/2 Hour - 35.00 1/4 Hour - 20.00	**TIME RATES** *Exclusive of Talent*	*NIGHT—7 P. M. to 12 M.* 1 Hour - $100.00 1/2 Hour - 65.00 1/4 Hour - 35.00
MORNING AIR MAIL 7 to 9 A. M. $5.00 per Broadcast Minimum Contract—12 Broadcasts *Above features can be used on alternating days.*	**DAILY FEATURES** (*Except Sunday*) **VARIETIES** DAILY—12 to 12.30 P. M. 5.30 to 6 P. M. 10 to 10.15 P. M. $75.00 weekly—18 Broadcasts Minimum Contract—1 week *Each Broadcast is interspersed by musical selections furnished by staff orchestra. No records.*	COMB. AIR MAIL and VARIETIES DAILY { 7 to 9 A. M. 12 to 12.30 P. M. { 5.30 to 6 P. M. 10 to 10.15 P. M. $100 weekly—24 Broadcasts Minimum Contract—1 week
ANNOUNCEMENTS AFTER 7 P. M. (75 words) $10 per Broadcast—Minimum 12 Broadcasts	**SPECIAL FEATURES** **ELECTRICAL TRANSCRIPTIONS** *Rates Furnished Upon Application* *TALENT BUREAU MAINTAINED FOR FURNISHING TALENT OF EVERY DESCRIPTION.*	POLITICAL, CHURCH, SOCIAL FUNCTIONS Rates Furnished Upon Application
13 weeks................Net 26 weeks................5%	**DISCOUNTS** 15% Agency Commission Allowed Recognized Advertising Agencies ON TIME ONLY — NOT ON TALENT *Discounts Allowed on Time Contracts Only.*	39 weeks ....10% 52 weeks 15%
EDGAR F. VOELCKER, General Manager.	EUGENE MARTINET, Director.	DAVIS MAYHORNE, Sales Manager.

This WFBR rate card, from September 1, 1930, reveals that businesses could buy an hour on the air—known as block time—for $60, an amount equal to nearly $900 today. At that time, the station broadcast at 1270 KC, from the eighth floor of the Chesapeake Bank Building, 7 St. Paul Street. (Courtesy National Capital Radio & Television Museum.)

As Advertised on

WITH

AM 1230

Tom Tinsley, owner of WITH, also had a station in Richmond, WLEE. Both used the same distinctive logo, reportedly a clean-shaven depiction of the Greek god Zeus. WITH resurrected the logo in the mid-1990s. (Author's collection.)

"The Great One" visited Channel 2. Jackie Gleason dropped by WMAR in 1962, most likely to promote his CBS variety series. A fixture on Saturday nights, Gleason was one of the network's biggest stars through the 1960s. He trained to the city from New York due to his fear of flying. (Courtesy John Ziemann.)

Baltimore's fourth television station was also it's first on the UHF (Ultra High Frequency) band. WMET broadcast from the former Avalon Theatre on Park Heights Avenue beginning in 1967. But transmission power was low and the station could only broadcast in black and white. More of a novelty than a legitimate competitor to WMAR, WJZ, and WBAL, Channel 24 went off the air in 1972. All that remains is the station's identification slide. (Courtesy Gary Michaels.)

WBAL general manager Brent Gunts (fourth from left, dark suit), accompanied Hearst Corporation, station, and city officials for groundbreaking ceremonies for their new building in Woodberry, at what would soon be referred to as "Television Hill." WBAL AM, FM, and TV moved in to their new facility in 1962. (Courtesy National Capital Radio & Television Museum.)

In its prime, WBMD aired the "Top Gun" jingle package while beaming country music to listeners at 750 AM and 105.7 FM. Programmer Clark West spent nearly a half century at the helm of the station, which did remote broadcasts from a pickup truck with a shell that resembled a log cabin. The station was located in Towson when this undated photograph was taken. (Courtesy Tom Conroy.)

Before the days of nonstop broadcasting, TV stations would sign off overnight and return to the air early the next morning. Viewers would hear a continuous tone and see a test pattern, like this one for WBAL, prior to the start of the day's programming. (Courtesy WBAL-TV.)

Print ads such as this one for WITH ran in industry trade publications, such as *Broadcasting Magazine*, and were designed to attract national sponsors. In the late 1950s and early 1960s, WITH went head-to-head with WCAO for young listeners and advertising dollars. (Courtesy National Capital Radio & Television Museum.)

WFBR's 25th anniversary celebration in June 1947 filled the house at the historic Lyric Theatre. Gatherings such as this demonstrated the lasting popularity of local radio, despite the emerging new medium of television. Lines outside of studios for a seat in the audience were common. (Courtesy National Capital Radio & Television Museum.)

WPOC was established in 1974 when Nationwide Communications, a subsidiary of Nationwide Insurance, purchased easy-listening WFMM. Adopting a country music format, WPOC buried its only local competitor, 95.9 WISZ-FM in Glen Burnie, within two years. (Courtesy Tom Conroy.)

This building, at 5200 Moravia Road, housed the offices and studios of 750 WBMD-AM and 105.7, which began as WBMD-FM. Over the years, the AM would switch from country to religious and ethnic programming. The FM was WKTK from 1977 to 1982. The other two stations, WPTX and WMDM, served Southern Maryland. (Courtesy Tom Conroy.)

This April 1937 photograph shows storm damage to WFBR's tower in Orangeville. As a result, the station relocated its transmission equipment to Waterview Avenue, on the Middle Branch of the Patapsco River. (Courtesy National Capital Radio & Television Museum.)

Each year, when "The Greatest Show on Earth" came to town, the elephants would be paraded from Camden Station, along Howard Street, and on to Lexington Market. Radio and television stations took full advantage of the crowd-pleasing event, not just covering it, but often being part of it, as WCBM did here in the early 1960s. (Courtesy National Capital Radio & Television Museum.)

Lite FM WLIF was formerly WAQE and WTOW-FM. Studios, transmitter and tower were at the end of Hart Road, off Providence Road, in a converted former house. When WLIF's owner, JAG Communications, purchased WFBR in 1988, it moved that station into this building as well. Air studios were on the second floor, with production in the basement. (Photograph by the author.)

WBAL-TV signed on in 1948. This may be the most familiar of the station's many logos. It was used from the 1960s until 1981, when the station dropped its NBC affiliation in favor of CBS. (Courtesy WBAL-TV.)

Maryland Public Television was established by legislation in 1966. Ground was broken on June 5, 1968, for its headquarters building and studio, seen in this artist's rendering. Broadcasts began over Channel 67, WMPB-TV, in October 1969. (Courtesy Fran Minakowski, MPT.)

NOBODY PLAYS
☆ OLDIES LIKE ☆

Oldies Radio
WQSR
FM 105.7

BRITISH INVASION ☆ BEACH MUSIC ☆ MOTOWN
WITH BALTIMORE'S BEST PERSONALITIES

The station on 105.7 became WQSR in 1982. With its "Goodtime Oldies" musical format, it was an instant hit with local baby boomers. Personalities like Steve Cochran, Lou Krieger, and Steve Rouse enjoyed tremendous popularity, cashing in on their wit, musical expertise, and relatability. (Courtesy National Capital Radio & Television Museum.)

In the early days of broadcasting, nearly all on-air talent were organized, members of the American Federation of Television & Radio Artists. AFTRA, as it is known, is still around, now merged with the Screen Actors Guild (SAG). As Ed Graham recalls, when AFTRA struck against WFBR in 1959, these picketers were brought in from stations in DC for this demonstration. (Courtesy National Capital Radio & Television Museum.)

When Pan Am Clipper service began at Logan Field in Dundalk, it was a major event, attracting visitors and media alike. From left to right, Gladys Marsheck, Virginia Echols, Louise and Antoinette Chell pose with the WFBR mobile van in 1937. Logan was the city's first airport. (Courtesy Dundalk-Patapsco Neck Historical Society Museum.)

Guy Erway founded WAYE in 1955. Offices and studios were in the Dundalk Village Shopping Center. The station later occupied space on North Charles Street and in the penthouse at Sutton Place. Erway is standing at the center. (Courtesy Dundalk-Patapsco Neck Historical Society Museum.)

The Television Hill candelabra tower, an engineering marvel for its time, was a great example of businesses working together for the greater good. All three television stations contributed to the cost of construction in 1959. The structure was designed by then-WJZ engineer Benjamin Wolfe, seen here kneeling at the right. (Courtesy Marian Wolfe Shuman.)

As a Top 40 rock 'n' roll station from the late 1950s, WCAO's share of the listening audience was challenged but never surpassed until improved FM technology allowed WLPL to slip past "the Big 60" around 1969. WCAO switched to country music in 1982. (Courtesy Tom Conroy.)

After more than a decade in The Sun Building downtown, WMAR began work on its own facility in 1962. "Television Park," as it was dubbed, was completed a year later, at 6400 York Road. (Courtesy John Ziemann.)

In the 1970s and 1980s, WFBR, then a Top 40 station, had Orioles baseball broadcasts, plus some incredibly talented personalities. Pete "the Flying Dutchman" Berry, "Commander" Jim Morton, Larry "Old Dirty Shirt" Walton, and the irrepressible Johnny Walker all contributed to "Mad Radio 13" and some of the best personality-driven radio anywhere. (Courtesy National Capital Radio & Television Museum.)

Its glory days behind it, WCAO's Pikesville facility was decidedly modest compared to the station's early days in the Upton Mansion. WXYV, originally WCAO-FM, has carried the WQSR call letters since 2001. (Courtesy Tom Conroy.)

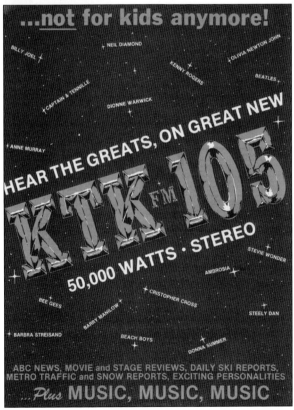

Hard rock fans celebrated when Key Broadcasting's WBMD-FM switched off the country music in 1971, in favor of "progressive" rock as WKTK. A few years later, however, it flipped to disco for two years before finally going to an oldies format in 1979. The calls would change to WQSR in 1982. (Courtesy National Capital Radio & Television Museum.)

This WBAL logo incorporated all three media—AM, FM, and TV—and dates from around 1961. WBAL-FM was originally WFDS until 1960. Since 1977, the station's been WIYY, 98 Rock, repeatedly recognized as one of the top rock stations in the nation. (Courtesy WBAL-TV.)

DUNDALK'S NEW
RADIO STATION
WAYE

is looking for an unusual girl
for receptionist - secretary.

CAN YOU QUALIFY?

Single, 21 - 30, outstanding personality, neat and
attractive. Good salary. In ultra modern office.

**Phone ATwater 4-3800
between 2 and 4 P.M. for appointment.**

Here is an early "Help Wanted" advertisement for WAYE. Needless to say, requirements such as these would be unacceptable today. 860 AM carried the WAYE call letters until 1984, when it became WBGR. (Courtesy Dundalk-Patapsco Neck Historical Society Museum.)

Here is the last WFBR studio control board. When JAG Communications bought WFBR from Baltimore Radio Show in 1988, all operations were moved from Twentieth Street to WLIF on Hart Road. Independent operation ceased in January 1990, when the station became WLIF-AM, a 100 percent simulcast of the FM. After 66 years (plus two more as WEAR), WFBR was gone. (Photograph by the author.)

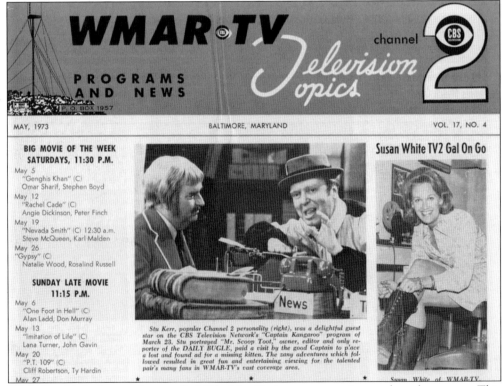

WMAR published a newsletter called *Television Topics* to promote its people and programs. This installment featured Stu Kerr portraying "Scoop Toot," a semi-regular character on the national *Captain Kangaroo* program. Susan White was also on the front page of this edition from May 1973. (Courtesy John Ziemann.)

WWIN TOP 40 tunes for the week

FEBRUARY 10, 1964

	TITLE	ARTIST	LABEL	LAST WEEK
1.	CAN'T WAIT TO SEE MY BABY	Baby Washington	SUE	4
2.	OH BABY DON'T YOU WEEP	James Brown	KING	3
3.	UM UM UM UM UM UM	Major Lance	OKEH	1
4.	TALKING ABOUT MY BABY	The Impressions	ABC	2
5.	YOU'LL NEVER WALK ALONE	The Blue Belles	PARKWAY	5
6.	STANDING AT CROSSROADS	The Supremes	MOTOWN	11
7.	I KNOW I'M SURE	James Conwell	4J	8
8.	I CAN'T STAND IT	Soul Sisters	SUE	9
9.	HERE'S A HEART	The Diplomats	AROCK	7
10.	ANYONE WHO HAD A HEART	Dionne Warwick	SCEPTER	6
11.	NEED TO BELONG	Jerry Butler	VEE JAY	14
12.	WHO DO YOU LOVE?	The Sapphires	SWAN	17
13.	VAYA CON DIOS	The Drifters	ATLANTIC	21
14.	FORGIVE THEN FORGET	Jay Wiggens	IPG	--
15.	IF SOMEBODY TOLD YOU	Anna King	SMASH	10
16.	JUMP FOR JOY	Charlie Lucas	ENJOY	18
17.	GOTTA FIND A WAY	Theresa Lindsey	CORRECTONE	25
18.	NOBODY BUT YOU GIRL	Chuck Leonard	CRACKERJACK	36
19.	FORGET ABOUT ME	Carolyn Crawford	MOTOWN	28
20.	THINK NOTHING ABOUT IT	Gene Chandler	CONSTELLATION	
21.	DANCING TO KEEP FROM CRYING	The Miracles	TAMLA	12
22.	SEND YOU BACK TO GEORGIA	Jimmy Shaw	WAND	22
23.	ASK ME	Inez Fox	SUE	15
24.	AS LONG AS I KNOW	The Marvelettes	TAMLA	13
25.	GOOD NEWS	Sam Cooke	RCA VICTOR	32
26.	IN A LITTLE WHILE	Chet Ivey	BEE CEE	16
27.	CAN YOUR MONKEY DO THE DOG?	Rufus Thomas	STAX	37
28.	IS IT ALL OVER?	The Townsmen	HERALD	19
29.	WHAT YOU WANT ME TO DO	Etta James	ARGO	30
30.	I WISH YOU LOVE	Gloria Lynne	EVEREST	38
31.	CASTLES IN THE SAND	Little Stevie	TAMLA	--
32.	OLD FATHER TIME	Millie Foster	2CF	33
33.	STRANGE THINGS HAPPENING	Little Jr. Parker	DUKE	--
34.	LIVE WIRE	Martha & Vandellas	MOTOWN	--
35.	I LOVE YOU	Ed Townsend	MAXX	--
36.	I LOVE HIM SO	The Bouquets	MALA	--
37.	HI HEEL SNEAKERS	Tommy Tucker	CHECKER	--
38.	RENTED TUXEDO..(EX-PIK)	H. B. Barnum	IMPERIAL	--
39.	HE'LL HAVE TO GO	Solomon Burke	ATLANTIC	--
40.	MORNING TEARDROPS	Benny Turner	SKYMAC	40

WWIN PICK OF WEEK: "I'M JUST LOOKING FOR LOVE"
By The Relatives on Almont

Winning Albums: "Apollo Saturday Night" on Atco
"Basie-Easin' It" on Roulette
"Jerry Butler-Need To Belong" on
Vee Jay

LARRY DEAN
6-9AM&12-2PM

KITTY BROADY
9AM-12NOON

AL JEFFERSON
2-7 PM

KELSON FISHER
8PM-1AM

JOCKO HENDERSON
10-11PM

MR. V.
1-6AM

RADIO 140 WWIN 24 HRS. A DAY
NOW FOUR TIMES MORE POWER!

WWIN debuted in 1951, and was the starting place for the careers of Jack Edwards, Ed Graham, and Jack Dawson. In the early 1960s, the station went to an African American format under the leadership of "long, lean Larry Dean" and, like many stations, published a weekly Top 40 chart. This one was from February 10, 1964. (Author's collection.)

Promotional items were commonplace among broadcast stations, primarily to attract advertisers. WCAO published this booklet around 1940, when just four radio stations existed in the city. (Courtesy National Capital Radio & Television Museum.)

Grading was underway in this early-1960s photograph of the site that would become WBAL's headquarters. Soon, Pete the Pirate, P.W. Doodle, *Pinbusters*, and J.P. Puppet (among others) would call it home. (Courtesy WBAL-TV.)

WFBR made one last attempt to revive music, news, and personalities on the AM band in 1988 and 1989. Competing for WQSR's listeners, WFBR featured music from the mid-1950s up to, but not including, the British Invasion. The personnel included the venerable Jack Edwards, Ira Siegel, and Bob Moke. On Labor Day 1989, in a cost-cutting measure, WFBR switched to an all-business format, with programming provided via satellite. (Author's collection.)

Another WMAR newsletter—this one from October 1957—celebrated the station's 10th anniversary. The photograph features the WMAR sign, affixed to the Sunpapers Building at Charles and Redwood Streets, with the former Mathieson Building on Light Street, where WMAR's transmission tower can be seen. (Courtesy John Ziemann.)

The Baltimore Radio Show placed this industry trade advertisement, touting the combined listenership of WFBR and WBKZ, formerly WISZ-FM. WBKZ, or Z-96, was sold to Belvedere Broadcasting Company in the early 1980s. Today, the station is top-rated WWIN-FM. (Courtesy National Capital Radio & Television Museum.)

Two

SHOWS

Local radio and television stations have presented every manner of show since the 1920s. News and music immediately come to mind, followed by sporting events. The earliest broadcast of an Orioles game is believed to have been in 1925 on WCBM when, using wire reports, an announcer named Stewart Kennard described the game. The opponent that day was Louisville.

High Jinks was a musical comedy program from the 1930s on WBAL, featuring Garry Moore among others. Moore also hosted an early show called *Treasure Hunt*, with WBAL colleague Walter Linthicum.

One of the better known shows on WFBR was *Club 1300*, a talent competition hosted by Bill Lefevre, among others. *Melody Ballroom* was another long-term WFBR offering. Bob Landers was its first host, and Joe Knight its last.

Early risers woke up to *Morning Musical Clock* on WCAO, while WBAL listeners tuned in to *Around the Breakfast Table*. *Morning in Maryland* got WFBR listeners up and moving. Later, it was *Wake Up, Baltimore* with Buddy Deane on WITH.

Dialing for Dollars began in 1939 on WCBM, where Homer Todd served as the first "Mr. Fortune." For a time, it was simulcast on Channel 2 as well, before WCBM dropped it in the early 1960s, leaving WMAR to air it solo through 1977.

Newell Warner directed and hosted *Children's Theatre of the Air* and other programs for youngsters on WCBM from the 1930s. His brother Henry did *Dream Children* on WCAO and WBAL.

Charles Purcell hosted a long-running overnight show on WCAO called *Nocturne*. Then there was *Mollie Martin* on WBAL, played by Dorothy Cotton and, later, Melva Forsythe. And over on WFBR, Henry Hickman hosted *Quiz of Two Cities*, pitting contestants from Baltimore and Washington against each other.

When TV came along, viewers watched Hugh Hefner's brother Keith host *Mr. Toby's Tip-Top Merry-Go Round* on WAAM, *Date To Dance* with Jay Grayson on WBAL, and wrestling hosted by Bailey Goss.

As time went on, they would tune in *Pogo's Cartoon Circus* on Channel 24, catch *Conference Call* on WFBR, join Brent Gunts and Jay Grayson for WBAL-TV's *One O'Clock Show*, enjoy *Maryland Weekend* on Channel 67 with Bob "the Balding Eagle" Callahan, and listen to great jazz on *The Harley Show*.

Your favorites "Kitty and Bingo" of the Open Mike program heard over W B A L every Tuesday, Thursday and Saturday 12.15-12.30.

WBAL's *Kitty & Bingo* were, in reality, Kitty Dierken and Thomas Garrison Morfitt, later known as Garry Moore. Their *Open Mic* program aired three times a week in the late 1930s, and both were also members of "The WBAL Radio Players." Dierken later hosted a 45-minute show on WAAM-TV selling all manner of items, while Moore went on to national radio and TV fame. (Courtesy Bob Bell.)

PROGRAM HI-LITES

GOOD LISTENING...AROUND THE CLOCK

SUNDAY AFTERNOON
2:00 P.M. This Week Around The World
*2:30 P.M. Best Loved Melodies
3:00 P.M. Lassie
3:15 P.M. Sam Pettengill
3:30 P.M. Sammy Kaye
4:30 P.M. Metropolitan Auditions

★

MONDAY AFTERNOON
*1:05 P.M. Club 1300
*2:00 P.M. Shoppin' Fun
2:30 P.M. Bride and Groom
*4:30 P.M. Every Woman's Hour

★

TUESDAY MORNING
*6-9 A.M. Morning in Maryland
9:00 A.M. Breakfast Club
10:00 A.M. My True Story
11:45 A.M. Ted Malone

MOST POPULAR DAYTIME HOUR
Good music, homey, friendly personalities and loads of gifts make this Baltimore's most popular daytime hour!

CLUB 1300
DAILY 1:05 P.M.

★

WEDNESDAY EVENING
7:30 P.M. Lone Ranger
8:00 P.M. Mayor of the Town
8:30 P.M. Vox Pop
9:00 P.M. Abbott & Costello
9:30 P.M. Groucho Marx
10:00 P.M. Bing Crosby
*10:30 P.M. Quiz of 2 Cities

*Produced in the Studios of WFBR.

THURSDAY MORNING
10:25 A.M. Betty Crocker Magazine
10:45 A.M. Dorothy Kilgallen
11:00 A.M. Breakfast in Hollywood
11:30 A.M. Galen Drake

★

FRIDAY EVENING
8:00 P.M. The Fat Man
8:30 P.M. This is your FBI
9:00 P.M. Break the Bank
9:30 P.M. The Sheriff
10:00 P.M. Boxing Bouts

★

SATURDAY EVENING
8:30 P.M. Famous Jury Trials
9:00 P.M. Gang Busters
9:30 P.M. Murder & Mr. Malone
10:00 P.M. Professor Quiz

WFBR
1300 ON YOUR DIAL

AMERICAN BROADCASTING COMPANY

WFBR's program schedule in the late 1940s included national programs like *Abbott & Costello*, *The Lone Ranger*, and *Bing Crosby*, plus local shows like *Morning in Maryland*, *The Breakfast Club*, *Every Woman's Hour*, and the very popular *Club 1300*. (From the author's collection.)

One of Baltimore's earliest children's television programs was *Paul's Puppets*. Bernard and Edith Paul had been performing with marionettes since the 1930s, and were responsible for puppetry, writing, costumes, and all aspects of their shows. Hutzler's Department Store was the program's longtime sponsor on WBAL-TV. (Author's collection.)

In 1938, Douglas "Wrong Way" Corrigan paid a visit to Logan Field in Dundalk, attracting an impressive-sized crowd in the process. Pictured from left to right are (first row) local reporters Walter Hough, G.H. Pouder, and WFBR's Stewart Kennard; (second row) aviator Glenn L. Martin, American Airlines flight attendant Frances Kry, and Corrigan. (Courtesy Dundalk-Patapsco Neck Historical Society Museum.)

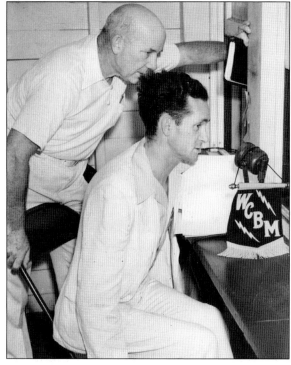

Teen Canteen was an early music and dance program on WBAL-TV. Hosted by John Bowman, it was one of several local shows aimed at young people, including *Hi-Time*, *WAAMboreee*, and *The Buddy Deane Show* on Channel 13; *The Collegians*, a local talent show on WMAR; and later, *The Kerby Scott Show* on Channel 11. (Courtesy WBAL-TV.)

The International League Baltimore Orioles games were first broadcast in the 1920s on WCBM. The announcers at the mic in this 1940 photograph are Newell Warner (left) and Lee Davis. In a long career at WCBM, Warner wore many hats, including that of religious programming director. (Courtesy National Capital Radio & Television Museum.)

Newell Warner was master of ceremonies for this 1946 broadcast of *Children's Theatre*, sponsored by Rensie Watches. The program originated from WCBM's studios in the Sears Community House on North Avenue and Broadway, formerly the Samuel Ready School for Girls. Warner, who was also director of the show, joined WCBM in 1931. (Courtesy National Capital Radio & Television Museum.)

Long associated with local sports programming, Baltimore's National Brewing Company sponsored *The National Sports Parade* on WMAR. One of the station's first shows, it was initially hosted by Jim McManus ("Jim McKay"). Bailey Goss took over following McManus's departure to CBS in 1950. His guest on this episode from the 1950s was Baltimore Colts defensive back Don Shula. (Courtesy John Ziemann.)

The Big Pud was one of many children's show characters created by Royal Parker. Born Royal Pollokoff in 1929, the Baltimore native got his start at the old WASA-AM in Havre de Grace before moving to WAAM-TV in 1951. The "Pud" name was inspired by Royal Pudding. (Courtesy Royal Parker.)

Ed Bakey was a Havre de Grace native who epitomized the expression "local boy makes good." As Pop Pop on Channel 13, Bakey enjoyed instant success with the bubble-gum crowd, so much so that he took the character north and became Tommy Seven on New York's WABC-TV. That led to a long career in movies and television, in voiceovers, and even the Broadway stage. As Eddie Greensleeves, he recorded an album called Humorous Folksongs by Greensleeves, and brought the character to life as a frequent guest on Jack Paar's Tonight Show. (Courtesy Royal Parker.)

This newspaper ad from the late 1940s promoted WFBR's evening programming, from the fledgling ABC Radio Network. Formerly the Blue Network, it was originally one of two radio networks (the other Red) from NBC before a court-ordered divestiture in 1942 following anti-trust litigation. (Author's collection.)

In a studio that had once been the *Baltimore Sun* City Room, Dave Stickle, seated at the desk far left, anchored WMAR's 1952 election coverage. The unsophisticated props and graphics of the day included hand-written vote totals posted on simple plywood backdrops. The remaining personnel were not identified. (Courtesy John Ziemann.)

Dated 1946, this image features Newell Warner, again hosting WCBM's *Children's Theatre of the Air*, sponsored this time by Post Toasties cereal, a bowl of which was served to each youthful audience member. The chalkboard at the left promotes another WCBM production, *House of Mystery*. (Courtesy National Capital Radio & Television Museum.)

The year was 1952, and the venue Municipal Stadium, where future Baseball Hall of Fame broadcaster Chuck Thompson was conducting an interview of International League Orioles player Marv Rackley for WMAR-TV. Thompson, who covered the Orioles on WITH-AM from 1949 to 1953, also hosted a jazz music program on the station. (Courtesy John Ziemann.)

Conference Call, a daily issues-oriented public affairs program, was the brainchild of WFBR president and general manager Harry Shriver. In this October 1962 photograph, panelists were, from left to right, moderator Bill Jaeger, newsmen Lou Corbin and Ted Beinert, and Shriver. (Courtesy National Capital Radio & Television Museum.)

"Introducing Bozo, The World's Most Famous Clown!" And locally, Bozo was Stu Kerr, one of Baltimore's most beloved TV and radio personalities. This picture, from Halloween 1961, shows Kerr at the far right making his grand entrance into the "Big Top." The show's villain was a character wearing a gorilla's mask named Somerset. (Courtesy John Ziemann.)

Pinbusters was a weekly duckpin bowling program for youngsters, hosted by John Bowman, and airing on WBAL-TV. Boys and girls in three different age groups competed for trophies every Saturday evening. A Bert Claster production, *Pinbusters* originated from the old Recreation Lanes on Howard Street until WBAL moved to Television Hill. (Courtesy Kathy Bowman Young.)

The Buddy Deane Show was nothing short of legendary. Airing on Channel 13 from 1957 to 1964, it was so popular that WJZ chose to run it instead of Dick Clark's nationally televised *American Bandstand*, which ABC aired at the same hour. In this undated image, guests included deejay Paul "Fat Daddy" Johnson, and Smokey Robinson and the Miracles. The races were not permitted to dance together, so on this day, African American teens were on the show. (Courtesy Don Lehnhoff.)

From 1962 to 1966, as Lorenzo the Tramp on WJZ-TV, Gerry Wheeler was responsible for a huge increase in the sale of Tootsie Pops and copies of Boots Randolph's "Yakety Sax." Lorenzo, who never spoke but managed to communicate with viewers and an off-screen announcer—usually Jerry Turner—was responsible for many a local child missing the morning bus to school. Wheeler died in 2013. (Courtesy Bob Bell.)

When Lary and Nancy Lewman came to Baltimore from Terre Haute, Indiana, in 1959, they hosted *What's New, with The Lewmans* on WBAL-TV. Commenting in 2001, Lary said of the show, "There was no evidence in the rating book that anyone even in the building was watching it," and the show ended in August 1960. (Courtesy WBAL-TV.)

During the 1940s, educator Frank Woodfield presented *The Hobby Club of the Air*, also known as *Uncle Frank's Hobby Club*. Aimed at youngsters considered to be at risk for delinquency, the program aired Saturdays on WFBR and was sponsored by Rice's Bakery. (Courtesy National Capital Radio & Television Museum.)

Rhea Feikin's first local television appearance was as a 16-year-old on the first telecast of *Hi-Time* on WAAM-TV. She scored her own program, an educational show called *Betty Better Speech*, a few years later on WBAL. That was followed by *Miss Rhea & Sunshine* with local puppeteer Cal Schumann, where she showed off more than 120,000 ice-cream sticks collected for charity. (Courtesy WBAL-TV.)

It was an exciting day in 1950 when Friendship Airport opened in Anne Arundel County, replacing Baltimore Municipal Airport—also known as Harbor Field—in Dundalk. Covering the event for WFBR were Henry Hickman (left) and Lou Corbin. (Courtesy National Capital Radio & Television Museum.)

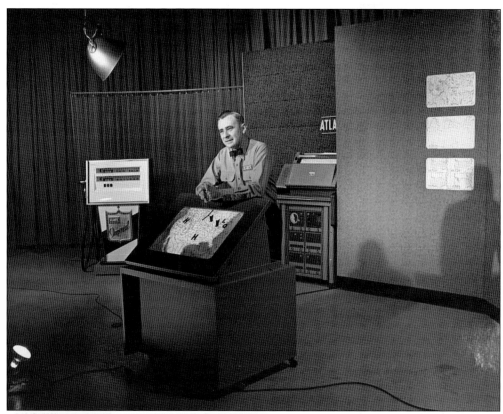

In the early 1960s, Al Herndon, wearing a gas station attendant's jumpsuit, presented the weather during WBAL-TV newscasts, sponsored by Atlantic gasoline. The Gulf Oil Company took over later in the decade, with Rhea Feikin providing the forecast, accompanied by J.P. Puppet for comic relief. (Courtesy WBAL-TV.)

When WBAL-TV acquired the rights to *The Mickey Mouse Club*, they called on Royal Parker to create a new character to host. Parker, who had just joined the station from WJZ, came up with "P.W. Doodle" and made him a news boy, with the reason being he himself had sold newspapers as a child to help support his family after the death of his father. (Courtesy Royal Parker.)

PLATE 11 - SCHOLASTIC SPORTS
Mayor McKeldin and Tom Harmon, of football fame, endorse WCBM trophy awards in four major high school sports.

In the 1940s, Mayor Theodore McKeldin and football great Tom Harmon ("Old 98") appeared on WCBM to promote that station's recognition of high school athletes. McKeldin would go on to become governor in 1951 and then return for another term as Baltimore's mayor in 1963. Harmon became a network sports broadcaster. His son Mark would become famous on the TV series *NCIS*. (Courtesy National Capital Radio & Television Museum.)

ENJOY weekday bowling fun! SPARETIME 10 AM your host *Tom Cole* WBAL-TV 11 BALTIMORE

Before he became a staff announcer and host of *Spare Time* on WBAL-TV, Tom Cole worked in radio, first for WAQE, then WCBM. *Spare Time, The Bowling Show Starring The Ladies* aired weekday mornings at 10 during much of the 1960s. After leaving television in the 1970s, the Loyola College graduate sold real estate. (Courtesy WBAL-TV.)

Conference Call landed former Georgia governor Jimmy Carter (right) as a guest in 1976. Carter, who would become the nation's 39th president the following January, faced questions from, left to right, WFBR president and general manager Harry Shriver and newsmen Tom Marr and Ron Matz. (Courtesy National Capital Radio & Television Museum.)

Mr. Poplolly was another creation of Royal Parker during his years at Channel 13. A streetcar conductor, the set consisted of a "Toonerville Trolley" that rocked from side to side when the host shifted his weight. After Parker left for WBAL in 1962, he prepared to resurrect Mr. Poplolly for Channel 11. However, WJZ nixed the plan, claiming the character was their property. (Courtesy Royal Parker.)

This print ad, from around 1960, promoted WJZ's morning lineup: *Patches*, *The Jack Wells Show*, and *The Popeye Club*. Patches was Jarrett Spotswood Lickle, who, with wife Liz and their collie dogs Valley and Sage, played guitar and sang songs like "The Big Rock Candy Mountain" and "I Knew An Old Lady Who Swallowed A Fly." He died in 2012 at the age of 87. (Courtesy National Capital Radio & Television Museum.)

PHIL CRIST   RALPH POWERS

Phil Crist (left) and Ralph Powers hosted *Morning in Maryland* weekdays on WFBR, a show that aired during the 1940s and 1950s. Judging by this posed publicity photograph, only one (Crist) was a "morning person." He later became the station's record librarian. (Courtesy National Capital Radio Television Museum.)

"Ahoy buccaneers. Come aboard, me hearty!" So began each episode of *Pete the Pirate* on WBAL-TV, every afternoon from 1960 to 1965. Lary Lewman was the man behind the beard. Pete's unseen adversary was Captain Awfulmean. (Courtesy WBAL-TV.)

"Shazam!" The janitor meets the Marine. In 1964, while on a promotional tour to CBS affiliate stations, Gomer Pyle (Jim Nabors) paid a call on WMAR-TV, where he was greeted by *The Early Riser*'s Stu Kerr. (Courtesy John Ziemann.)

The year was 1942, and Lou Corbin was at the WFBR mic doing a live remote broadcast from the basement restaurant of Brager's (later Brager-Gutman's) Department Store in downtown Baltimore. (Courtesy National Capital Radio & Television Museum.)

WBAL journalist Pam Fields, framed between a camera and the floor director, joined the station around 1970. In addition to her duties as a reporter, Fields was cohost of *North Star*, an African American public affairs program. Her father was baseball Hall of Famer Monte Irvin. (Courtesy Bruno Baran.)

Bert and Nancy Claster were producing variety shows at the Hippodrome when, in 1953, they decided to try television. The result was *Romper Room*, an in-studio classroom for preschoolers. Locally, it began on WBAL-TV, but over time moved to WJZ and then WMAR. Nationally franchised, there were more than 100 stations across the country airing their own *Romper Room*. (Courtesy WBAL-TV.)

TURNTABLE TIPS . . . .

Baltimore's original Hit Tune Survey!

WEEK ENDING JUNE 13

BUDDY DEANE'S TOP 50 RECORDS for the WEEK

WATCH THE BUDDY DEANE SHOW AFTERNOONS

CHANNEL *13

WJZ 13 TV

THIS WEEK	TITLE	ARTIST	LABEL	LAST WEEK
—1.	THE BATTLE OF NEW ORLEANS	Johnny Horton†	Columbia	1
—2.	PERSONALITY	Lloyd Price†	ABC-Par.	2
3.	DREAM LOVER	Bobby Darin†	Atco	4
—4.	WATERLOO	Stonewall Jackson†	Columbia	8
5.	LIPSTICK ON YOUR COLLAR	Connie Francis†	MGM	7
6.	MY HEART IS AN OPEN BOOK	Carl Dobkins†	Decca	12
7.	QUIET VILLAGE	Martin Denny	Liberty	3
—8.	LONELY BOY	Paul Anka†	ABC-Par.	16
—9.	KOOKIE, KOOKIE	Edward Byrnes	Warner Bros.	6
—10.	ONLY YOU	Franck Pourcel	Capitol	5
11.	GOODBYE, JIMMIE GOODBYE	Kathy Linden†	Felsted	17
—12.	ALONG CAME JONES	The Coasters†	Atco	23
13.	MELANCHOLY BABY	Tommy Edwards†	MGM	10
14.	SO FINE	The Fiestas†	Old Town	9
—15.	BOBBY SOX TO STOCKINGS	Frankie Avalon†	Chancellor	24
—16.	LITTLE DIPPER	Mickey Mozart	Roulette	15
17.	SOMETHING ON YOUR MIND	Big Jay McNeely†	Swingin'	22
—18.	THE HAPPY ORGAN	Dave Cortez†	Clock	11
19.	I KNOW	Perry Como	Victor-D&H	BB
20.	THE WONDER OF YOU	Ray Peterson†	Victor	34
21.	ENDLESSLY* b/w SO CLOSE	Brook Benton†	Mercury	21
22.	OH WHAT IT SEEMED TO BE	Bill Kenny	Tel	47
23.	WITH MY EYES WIDE OPEN	Patti Page	Mercury	33
24.	I'VE COME OF AGE	Billy Storm†	Columbia	14
—25.	DEDICATED TO THE ONE I LOVE	The Shirells	Sceptor	50
—26.	FRANKIE'S MAN JOHNNY	Johnny Cash	Columbia	13
27.	JUST KEEP IT UP	Dee Clark†	Abner	25
28.	GIDGET	James Darren†	Col Pix	43
29.	KANSAS CITY	Olson, Harrison Ballard	Chess, Fury King	27
— 30.	I WAITED TOO LONG	Lavern Baker†	Atlantic	45
—31.	BONGO ROCK *	Preston Epps†	Original	28
32.	GUESS WHO	Jesse Belvin†	Victor	18
—33.	YOUNG IDEAS	Chico Holiday†	Victor	29
34.	TALLAHASSEE LASSIE	Freddy Cannon†	Swan	30
35.	A TEENAGER IN LOVE	The Belmonts†	Laurie	20
36.	MONA LISA	Carl Mann†	Phillips	40
37.	LONELY TRAVELER*	Clint Miller	Big Top	31
—38.	TAKE A MESSAGE TO MARY	Everly Bros.†	Cadence	19
39.	LAVENDER-BLUE	Sammy Turner	Big Top	BB
40.	LITTLE BOY BLUE	Huelyn Duvall	Challenge	41
41.	BONAPARTE'S RETREAT	Billy Grammer†	Monument	49
—42.	THE CLASS	Chubby Checker†	Parkway	44
—43.	WALKIN' IN MY DREAMS	Chuck & Betty†	Decca	39
— 44.	POINTED TOE SHOES	Carl Perkins†	Columbia	35
45.	THIS I SWEAR	Skyliners†	Calico	36
46.	SMALL WORLD	Johnny Mathis†	Columbia	46
47.	SURE	Rod McKuen†	Decca	42
48.	HUSH A BYE	The Mystics	Laurie-Mar.	BB
49.	ONLY SIXTEEN	Sam Cooke†	Keen-G	BB
50.	WHAT A DIFFERENCE A DAY MAKES	Dinah Washington	Mercury-Z	BB

PROMISING NEW RELEASES

— TIGER	Fabian	Chancellor-Z
SINCE YOU'VE BEEN GONE	Clyde McPhatter	Atlantic-S
I ONLY HAVE EYES FOR YOU	The Flamingos	End-S
—FORTY MILES OF BAD ROAD	Duane Eddy	Jamie-S
A PRAYER AND A JUKEBOX	Little Anthony	End-S
I'M SO LONELY	J.B. Lloyd	Hi-J&F
M.T.A.	Kingston Trio	Capitol-Cap.
I'LL BE SATISFIED	Jackie Wilson	Brunswick-D
I'M COMING HOME	Marv Johnson	United Artist-Mar.
LOVER'S HYMN	Fontane Sisters	Dot-G
BACK IN THE U.S.A.	Chuck Berry	Chess-G
—CAP AND GOWN	Marty Robbins	Columbia-Col.

† Top Fifty Artists Who Have Appeared on The Buddy Deane Show.

No Baltimore deejay had more influence in the late 1950s and early 1960s than Buddy Deane. According to singer Johnny Tillotson, "When we had a new record, the first place we'd take it was *The Buddy Deane Show*." This copy of Buddy's top-50 songs of the week came from June 13, 1959. (Courtesy National Capital Radio & Television Museum.)

In addition to being coworkers at Channel 13, Jack Wells and Buddy Deane were both on the air at WITH. In 1996, the pair met up for the final time as part of WITH's 55th anniversary celebration. (Courtesy National Capital Radio & Television Museum.)

This was (obviously) an unguarded moment on the set of *P.W. Doodle*, around 1964, as Royal Parker grabbed a smoke while chatting with an unidentified technician. *Doodle* disappeared from the WBAL-TV lineup in 1965, when the station's *The Mickey Mouse Club* contract expired. (Courtesy Royal Parker.)

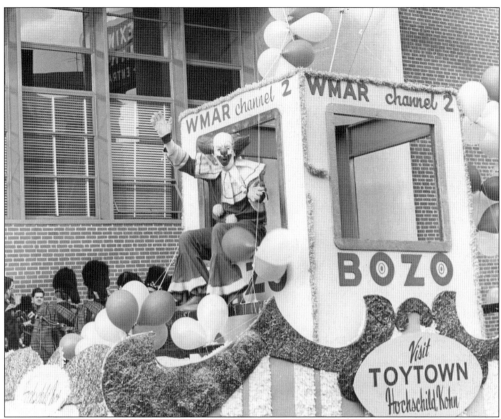

Hochschild Kohn department store was a sponsor of *The Bozo Show* on Channel 2. Here, star Stu Kerr shared a ride on the store's float during a parade in the early 1960s. Growing up in Yonkers, New York, Kerr was voted "most shy" by his high school senior class. (Courtesy John Ziemann.)

Hodge Podge Lodge aired from 1970 to 1977, and introduced children to animals and nature. Produced by Maryland Public Television and syndicated to other public stations across the country, it was hosted by "Miss Jean," Jean Worthley, accompanied by her Amazon parrot, Aurora. (Courtesy Fran Minakowski, MPT.)

Kerby "Kerbifer" Scott was a popular evening disc jockey on Top 40 station WCAO in the early- and mid-1960s. WDCA-TV, Channel 20 in Washington, hired Scott to host a daily dance show called *Wing Ding*. WBAL followed suit, giving Kerbifer his own show on Channel 11. (Courtesy WBAL-TV.)

The ground-breaking dramatic series *Our Street* premiered on Channel 67, WMPT, in October 1969. A total of 105 episodes were produced, and the series—about contemporary African American life in America—featured the television debut of locally born actor Howard E. Rollins Jr. (far right), who portrayed Slick Robinson. (Courtesy Fran Minakowski, MPT.)

What's Going On? View 2 ...and See!

WMAR-TV, CBS, CHANNEL 2, PROGRAMS — MAR., 1967

Sunday

8:30	Sunrise Semester
9:00	Underdog (C)
9:30	Gospel Singing Jubilee
10:00	Lamp Unto My Feet
10:30	Look Up and Live
11:00	Camera Three
11:30	Eleanor Nash Interviews
11:45	Your Family Doctor
12:00	Picture For a Sunday Afternoon
2:00	Medicine 1967 (C)
2:30	CBS Sports Spectacular (C)
4:00	CBS Children's Film Festival
5:00	Password (C)
5:30	Original Amateur Hour (C)
6:00	21st Century (C)
6:30	Death Valley Days (C)
7:00	Lassie (C)
7:30	It's About Time (C)
8:00	Ed Sullivan Show (C)
9:00	Smothers Brothers Comedy Hour (C)
10:00	Candid Camera (C)
10:30	What's My Line? (C)
11:00	Sunday News Report (C)
11:10	Weather Watch
11:15	Sports Roundup, John Mackey (C)
11:25	Sunday Snapshots
11:30	Channel 2 Sunday Theatre
1:25	Late News
1:30	Bible Reading

Daytime (Mon. thru Fri.)

6:30	Sunrise Semester
7:00	World at 7 A.M.
7:30	Gigantor
8:00	Captain Kangaroo
9:00	Romper Room (C)
9:30	Morning News (C)
9:40	Dialing For Dollars (C)
10:00	Divorce Court
11:00	Andy of Mayberry
11:30	Dick Van Dyke Show
12:00	Love of Life
12:25	Channel 2 Midday News (C)
12:30	Search For Tomorrow (C)
12:45	Guiding Light (C)
1:00	The Woman's Angle (C)
1:30	As the World Turns (C)
2:00	Password (C)
2:30	Art Linkletter's House Party (C)
3:00	To Tell the Truth (C)
3:25	Doctor's House Call
3:30	Edge of Night
4:00	Secret Storm
4:30	Superman
5:00	Twilight Movie
6:25	Early Report (C)
6:30	CBS Evening News, Walter Cronkite (C)
7:00	7 O'Clock Final (C)
7:15	What's With the Weather (C)
7:20	Sports Picture (C)

(C) Color

Monday Evening

7:30	Gilligan's Island (C)
8:00	Mr. Terrific (C)
8:30	The Lucy Show (C)
9:00	Andy Griffith Show (C)
9:30	Family Affair (C)
10:00	Divorce Court (C)
10:30	I've Got a Secret (C)
11:00	News Roundup (C)
11:10	Weather Time (C)
11:15	Sports Final (C)
11:20	Channel 2 Theatre
1:25	Late News
1:30	Bible Reading

Tuesday Evening

7:30	To Tell the Truth (C)
	NFL Action (C) eff. 3/21
8:00	Faith to Faith (C)
8:30	Red Skelton Hour (C)
9:30	Petticoat Junction (C)
10:00	CBS News Hour (C)
11:00	News Roundup (C)
11:10	Weather Time (C)
11:15	Sports Final (C)
11:20	Channel 2 Theatre
1:30	Late News
1:35	Bible Reading

Specials

Sunday, March 5. 11:30 p.m.-concl. — Doral Open Invitational Golf Tournament.

Monday, March 6, 9:30-11:00 p.m. — "Mark Twain Tonight!" — Hal Holbrook re-creates his memorable portrayal of the great American author and humorist in this 90-minute color special.

Saturday, March 11, 2:00-4:00 p.m. — National Invitation Tournament: First round game of 30th annual college basketball tournament from Madison Square Garden, in color.

Saturday, March 18, 2:00-4:00 p.m. — National Invitation Tournament Championship game; Championship college basketball game in color, from Madison Square Garden.

Sunday, March 26, 7:00-8:00 p.m. — "Marineland Carnival" — Art Carney, Jim Backus and Nancy Ames star in the fifth Easter Sunday edition of this comedy-variety special telecast in color from the world-famed aquatic part in Southern California

Wednesday Evening

7:30	Lost in Space (C)
8:30	Beverly Hillbillies (C)
9:00	Green Acres (C)
9:30	Gomer Pyle — USMC (C)
10:00	Danny Kaye Show (C)
11:00	News Roundup (C)
11:10	Weather Time (C)
11:15	Sports Final (C)
11:20	Channel 2 Theatre
1:25	Late News
1:30	Bible Reading

Thursday Evening

7:30	Coliseum (C)
8:30	My Three Sons (C)
9:00	CBS Thursday Night Movies (C)
11:00	News Roundup (C)
11:10	Weather Time (C)
11:15	Sports Final (C)
11:20	Channel 2 Theatre
1:10	Late News
1:15	Bible Reading

Friday Evening

7:30	Wild, Wild West (C)
8:30	Hogan's Heroes (C)
9:00	CBS Friday Night Movies (C)
11:00	News Roundup (C)
11:10	Weather Time (C)
11:15	Sports Final (C)
11:20	Friday's Big Movie
1:45	Late News
1:50	Bible Reading

Saturday

7:25	Early News
7:30	Mighty Mouse & Mighty Heroes (C)
8:00	Captain Kangaroo
9:00	Professor Kool and His Fun School (C)
9:30	Gigantor
10:00	Frankenstein Jr. & The Impossibles (C)
10:30	Space Ghost (C)
11:00	New Adventures of Superman (C)
11:30	Lone Ranger (C)
12:00	Road Runner (C)
12:30	The Beagles (C)
1:00	Tom & Jerry (C)
1:30	To be announced
2:00	College Basketball
4:00	Gadabout Gaddis (C)
4:30	Racing From Florida
5:00	Daktari (C)
6:00	Saturday's Top Movie
7:30	Jackie Gleason Show (C)
8:30	Mission: Impossible (C)
9:30	Pistols 'n' Petticoats (C)
10:00	Gunsmoke (C)
11:00	Big Movie of the Week
12:45	Second Feature
2:15	Late News
2:20	Lord's Prayer

This was the program lineup offered by WMAR-TV in the month of March 1967. In addition to shows from CBS, the station featured local favorites *Dialing for Dollars* and *Professor Kool & His Fun Skool*, both of which starred the venerable Stu Kerr. (Courtesy John Ziemann.)

Speaking of Stu Kerr, he was known here as Mr. Fortune, the genial host of the long-running *Dialing for Dollars*. He posed here behind the giant rotary telephone with cohost Sylvia Scott and the Uniformed Custodian, who kept watch over the pretend vault that housed the "Golden Cash Box." *Dialing for Dollars* originated on WCBM radio in 1939, with Homer Todd as the first Mr. Fortune. (Courtesy John Ziemann.)

Bowling for Dollars on WBAL was another Claster production, debuting in the 1960s as *The Bowling Bank*, and sponsored by American Beer. The first host was Tom Cole. He was succeeded by WCBM deejay Dennis Murray around 1972 and, finally, WCAO's Ron Riley, seen here wearing the fashions of the day. The show was renamed *Duckpins & Dollars* first and then, finally, *Bowling for Dollars* after one of the duckpin alleys was replaced with tenpins. (Courtesy WBAL-TV.)

Nearly a decade after he last sailed aboard the good ship *Fairwind* as Pete the Pirate, Lary Lewman, seen here in the foreground, surfaced in 1973 as host of *Consumer Survival Kit* on MPT. Created and produced by Vince Clews, the show was carried by PBS stations across the country. Lewman went on to a lucrative career in voiceover work. (Courtesy Fran Minakowski, MPT.)

DC-born Jim Simpson made the drive up the B-W Parkway in 1973 to join Rhea Feikin as cohost of *The Maryland State Lottery Show* on Channel 11. Simpson, who was the principal sportscaster for Washington's WRC-TV, previously hosted the nationwide *Sports in Action* on NBC, along with that network's coverage of hockey, baseball, tennis, golf, basketball, and the games of the old American Football League. (Courtesy WBAL-TV.)

Professor Kool's chief nemesis was Miss Spiderweb, seen here crouching on the right, helping herself to the unsuspecting educator's candy. Miss Spiderweb was WMAR technician John Ziemann, who, at the insistence of the American Federation of Television & Radio Artists union (of which he was not a member) could not speak and had to be covered from head to toe on camera. (Courtesy John Ziemann.)

This photograph was used in a 1976 advertisement promoting WMAR-TV's weekend news coverage. From left to right are Tom Marr, Dwight Smith, and Wayne Lynch. Lynch later taught news writing at the University of Washington-Tacoma and authored the book *Season of the 76ers*. (Courtesy John Ziemann.)

Another Maryland Public Television production, *MotorWeek*, premiered in October 1981. Created, produced, and hosted by John Davis, seen here at the center, the show is considered television's most respected automotive program, carried by more than 90 percent of America's public TV stations. (Courtesy Fran Minakowski, MPT.)

Club 1300 aired weekdays at 1 on WFBR. But on Saturdays, the show would hit the road, originating from Gwynn Oak Amusement Park, and the Dixie Ballroom. One of the show's early emcees was Erwin "Win" Elliott, who later became a top sportscaster for CBS. (Courtesy National Capital Radio & Television Museum.)

All eyes appeared to be on host Tom Cole as he prepared to take a shot at the duckpins during a break on *Spare Time*. Duckpin bowling was still hugely popular in the late 1960s, about the time this photograph was taken. Only about half the number of Maryland duckpin establishments that were around then are still open today. (Courtesy WBAL-TV.)

Toward the late 1960s, Gulf Oil began sponsoring weather segments on local television newscasts across the country. At WBAL-TV, Rhea Feikin was called upon to provide a fresh and entertaining slant to weathercasting, assisted by J.P. Puppet, who was, in reality, local puppeteer Cal Schumann. In the early 1970s, knowing they were about to be dismissed as part of a major newsroom overhaul, the pair walked off the set while on camera and in the midst of their segment. (Courtesy WBAL-TV.)

From 1946 to 1953, *Morning in Maryland* on WFBR was hosted by brothers Jim (left) and Phil Crist. The pair sang, did comedy routines, and even brushed their teeth on the air each morning, reminding listeners to do the same. Jim Crist died in 1980, and his brother passed in 1981. (Courtesy National Capital Radio & Television Museum.)

Unlike other TV kids' show hosts, Stu Kerr never attempted to change or disguise his voice. Whether he was the Early Riser, Bozo, Professor Kool, the Conductor (on *Caboose*—his last show for WMAR), or Commander Stuker on WNUV's *54 Space Corps*, the viewer always knew the man behind the makeup was Stu Kerr. (Courtesy John Ziemann.)

Dave Stickle (left) and George Rogers, seen here covering the 1968 elections, were WMAR's primary news anchors in the 1960s. Stickle had come from the *Sunpapers.* Rogers, who spent 10 years as Mr. Fortune on *Dialing for Dollars,* left the station around 1963 to host the nationally televised program *Shell's Wonderful World of Golf* but returned later. (Courtesy John Ziemann.)

Bill Herson (left) stayed busy doing mornings on WRC-AM in Washington, hosting *Coffee with Congress* on NBC radio, and working at WBAL-AM. Al Ross (right) was WBAL's popular morning man (*Around the Breakfast Table,* later renamed *The Al Ross Show*) from 1942 to 1955. (Courtesy National Capital Radio & Television Museum.)

Three

STARS

"Stars" may be overdoing it—"personalities" or "air talent" may be more appropriate. Whatever they are called, Baltimore's radio and television personnel have received an incredible amount of loyalty, attention, and affection from their audiences—so much so that many stayed in the area when other opportunities arose. The most successful understood that broadcasting, then as now, is a relationship business. These were the unpretentious ones who could communicate interest in and care for their audience, making the listener and/or viewer feel as if they were addressing only them. Arthur Godfrey understood this. Jim McKay recalled a 1950 meeting with Godfrey, after being hired away from WMAR by CBS. "The camera has an x-ray quality about it," said Godfrey. "It spots a phony every time." The lesson the 29-year-old McKay came away with was to be sincere and be yourself.

The list of local media personnel embraced by Baltimoreans could fill a volume in and of itself. From the early days, there was Garry Moore, Walter Linthicum, Newell Warner, Lee Davis, Galen Fromme, Harry Hickman, Jim and Phil Crist, Charles Purcell, Homer Todd, and Eddie Fenton.

In the middle of the 20th century came Stu Kerr, Nick Campofreda, Royal Parker, Bailey Goss, Chuck Thompson, Walt Teas, Tom O'Connor, Eddie Hubbard, Flo Ayres, Maurice "Hot Rod" Hulbert, Jack Wells, Gene Rayburn, Lee Case, Bill Lefevre, and Rolf Hertsgaard. Other standouts included Buddy Deane, Jack Gale, Jay Grayson, Keith McBee, Joe Knight, Larry Dean, Joe Croghan, Fred "Rockin' Robin" Robinson, Jack Edwards, and Baxter Ward.

In time, they were joined by Gerry Wheeler, Vince Bagli, Johnny Dark, Jerry Turner, Paul "Fat Daddy" Johnson, Bob McAllister, Johnny Contino, Al Sanders, Les "the Beard" Alexander, Ron Smith, Tom Marr, Randy Dennis, "Emperor" Paul Rodgers, Bob Moke, Ernie Boston, Sarah Fleischer, Mike James, Alan Field, Brian & O'Brien, Jon Miller, Dave Durian, Steve Rouse, Ray Davis, Tim Watts, Laurie DeYoung, Wayne Gruehn, Dick Ireland, "Commander" Jim Morton, Kirk McEwen, Lou Krieger, Kerby Scott, Johnny Walker, and more names than these pages can hold.

This c. 1961 WBAL-TV photograph features Jim Lyons and Rhea Feiken (with Sunshine) in the first row. The man in the first row, far right, is unidentified. Behind them are Rolf Hertsgaard, Al Herndon, and Joe Croghan. In the back at the far right is Lary Lewman, in character as "Pete the Pirate." The other two in the back row are unidentified. (Courtesy WBAL-TV).

Charles Purcell joined WCAO in 1937, and for the next 20 years, he cohosted a nightly show called *Nocturne*, broadcast from the Loew's Parkway and Century theatres. His career began in 1925 when, at age 14, he was billed as "Art Davis, the Ukulele Kid." Purcell died in 1981. (Courtesy National Capital Radio & Television Museum.)

EMPLOYEE'S PAYROLL CARD

NAME: *Arthur M Godfrey*

ADDRESS: ~~709 Pontiac Ave, Bklyn.~~ *1626 St. Paul St.*

PHONE NO.: *Curtis 0341 (Mrs. Snyder)*   DATE EMPLOYED: *2/3/30*

DUTIES: *Announcer*   SALARY WEEKLY: *18 00/100*

SALARIES *annual 936 00/100*

DATE	INCREASE	WEEKLY	ANNUALLY	DATE	INCREASE	WEEKLY	ANNUALLY
4/1/30	✓	*7.00*	*364.00*				
/29	✓	*10.00*	*520.00*		*10/18/30*		

Arthur Godfrey's WFBR payroll card from 1930 shows "the Old Redhead" was making $18 a week. Baltimore's Godfrey listed 1626 St. Paul Street as his residence. That site is now a parking lot for Pennsylvania Station. (Courtesy National Capital Radio & Television Museum.)

Godfrey was one of radio's first legitimate superstars. After leaving WFBR, he spent four years with NBC-owned WRC in Washington, then moved to CBS-owned WJSV, which became WTOP. His career in radio and television, and as a commercial pitch man, was legendary, and he continued his association with CBS until 1972. (Courtesy National Capital Radio & Television Museum.)

James McManus was writing for the *Sunpapers* when management made him the first face and voice on Baltimore television. He called the races from Pimlico, then a basketball game from the old Coliseum, the day WMAR signed on. He produced and hosted *The National Sports Parade* on Channel 2 before moving to CBS in New York in 1950, where his name was changed to Jim McKay. He became host of *ABC's Wide World of Sports* in 1961 and covered 12 Olympic games. Winner of numerous awards including a Peabody and 13 Emmys, Jim McKay died June 7, 2008. He was 86. (Courtesy Mary McManus Guba.)

Johnny Dark had talent, poise, versatility, knowledge, and sincerity. Born John Bennett in Cambridge, Massachusetts, in 1934, Johnny spent most of his career at WCAO, during both its Top 40 and country periods. He introduced the Beatles at their 1964 concert in Baltimore and coached the WCAO "Good Guys" basketball team. He died September 15, 2016. (Courtesy Tom Conroy.)

JOHNNY DARK
AFTERNOONS
WCAO
RADIO·60

The sportscasting tandem of Chuck Thompson (left) and Bill O'Donnell was in a league of its own. They did both the Orioles and Colts games in the 1960s and early 1970s, with Thompson eventually being enshrined in the broadcaster's wing of the Baseball Hall of Fame. O'Donnell came to Baltimore from Syracuse, where he called minor-league baseball and Orangemen sports. (Courtesy National Capital Radio & Television Museum.)

In 2002, then-84-year-old Brent Gunts recalled the day in 1928 when he accompanied a neighbor to his Sunday morning job at WCAO. Once there, the unnamed announcer put a record on the turntable, then exited to find a remedy for his hangover, leaving the untrained and slightly terrified 10-year-old to run things. In 1959, Gunts became vice president and general manager of WBAL-AM and TV, and WFDS-FM, which became WBAL-FM the following year. (Courtesy WBAL-TV.)

Galen Fromme joined WBAL in 1939, from WEEU in Reading, Pennsylvania. He was both versatile and talented, having won an earlier singing competition on the nationwide *Major Bowes' Amateur Hour* on NBC. At WBAL, all that talent and versatility would be put to the test. Fromme sang, acted, and ultimately became the station's news director, retiring in 1979 after 40 years with the station. (Courtesy National Capital Radio & Television Museum.)

Once a singer, dancer, and band leader, Maurice Hulbert moved into radio in 1949 at WDIA in Memphis, where he picked up the nickname "Hot Rod." Two years later, WITH was on the hunt for an African American air personality, and they wanted the best. They got Hot Rod, "the Bald Prince of the Air Waves." (Courtesy National Capital Radio & Television Museum.)

For 30 years, one of the busiest producer/directors at WBAL-TV was Joe Sullivan. His name could be seen in the credits, or heard from the booth announcer at the conclusion of *Pete the Pirate, Pinbusters, P.W. Doodle, Miss Rhea & Sunshine*, and other local shows. He began as a floor director at Channel 11 in the early 1950s. (Courtesy National Capital Radio & Television Museum.)

Brent Gunts produced *The Bob Jones Show* for WBAL-TV in the 1950s. Born in 1924, Jones was a 1949 graduate of George Washington University. He left Baltimore for his native Cincinnati in 1963, where he worked in news for WKRC radio and television. (Courtesy National Capital Radio & Television Museum.)

Dave Durian (left) came to WBAL-TV from Pittsburgh's KDKA in 1982, anchoring local newscasts until 1986. After two years at Maryland Public Television, Durian returned to WBAL in 1990, hosting the morning radio show through 2012. Rod Daniels (right) arrived in 1984 and spent more than 30 years in the anchor chair before retiring in 2015. (Courtesy WBAL-TV.)

Winston "Buddy" Deane was the morning show host on WITH when he was recruited to do a teen dance program on Channel 13. *The Buddy Deane Show* became legendary, airing until early 1964, and Deane was in great demand for emcee work and live shows throughout the region. Deane eventually returned to his native Arkansas, where he owned and operated six radio stations. *The Buddy Deane Show* was the inspiration for the 1988 film *Hairspray*. Active until the end, Deane died less than two months after his final public appearance, in 2003. He was 78. (Courtesy National Capital Radio & Television Museum.)

Benjamin Wolfe's name and face may not be familiar, but his love for radio and engineering changed the local broadcasting scene forever. Born January 6, 1914, the Baltimore native designed the Television Hill Candelabra Tower, and oversaw its construction in 1959. In time, he moved on to high-level jobs with Westinghouse Broadcasting, and the Post-Newsweek cluster. (Courtesy Marian Wolfe Shuman.)

It was another Bob Jones, not the one from the 1950s, who teamed with Jim West for the WBAL-AM morning show in 1979. Avoiding controversy and excess fluff, *Jones & West* had a consistently pleasant, highly listenable morning show. Years earlier, Jim West had been the radio play-by-play voice of hockey's Baltimore Clippers, after which time he spent eight years doing Blackhawks hockey and Cubs baseball at WGN-TV in Chicago. (Courtesy WBAL-TV.)

Paul Johnson had a rapid-fire delivery, multicultural appeal, and a really cool nickname. He was "Fat Daddy," the self-described "300 Pound King of Soul." Born in Baltimore in 1938, this Douglas High School and University of Maryland grad spent time on WSID, WWIN, and WITH, before leaving for Los Angeles, and a job in the music industry. Fat Daddy was just 40 when he died in 1978. (Courtesy Don Lehnhoff.)

John Courtland Bowman Jr. was a tall, mustachioed man. Gregarious by nature, he was also creative, coming up with interesting names for splits left by bowlers, such as "goalposts" for the 7-10, and "faith, hope, and charity," when the 5, 7, and 10 pins were left behind. His health deteriorated in the 1970s, and he was ultimately replaced by Royal Parker. John Bowman died at 63 on June 7, 1982, shortly after *Pinbusters* celebrated 25 years on the air. (Courtesy Kathy Bowman Young.)

"Your Knight of the Spinning Round Table" was Joe Knight. In a career that began in the 1940s sweeping the floors of a radio station in Great Bend, Kansas, Joseph Neidig was behind the mic before he got out of high school. From Kansas, he went to KDFA-AM in Amarillo, then KRMG-AM in Tulsa, where station manager R.B. Jones renamed him "Joe Knight." From there, it was on to WFBR in 1957 (he was the last host of *Melody Ballroom*), then WCBM from 1973 to 1983. (Courtesy National Capital Radio & Television Museum.)

Could a trumpet-playing, former railroad worker from Meridian, Mississippi, go on to become a beloved television news anchor? In the case of Jerry J. Joiner, the answer was yes. As Jerry Turner, he joined WJZ in August, 1962, replacing George Baumann as news anchor. Behind Turner, WJZ rose to the top of the local TV news ratings beginning in the late 1960s. Jerry Turner died of cancer at 58 on December 31, 1987. (Courtesy MARMIA.)

John Herbert ("Jack Edwards") got his start in local radio at WWIN in 1957. Since then, he's worked for just about every station in town—WCAO, WCBM, WYST, WITH, WQSR, and WFBR, where this photograph was taken over Labor Day weekend, 1989. (Photograph by the author.)

In 1964, after five years as a sports writer for the *Baltimore News-American*, Vince Bagli came to WBAL-TV. As sports director, he remained a fixture on Television Hill until retiring in 1995. His signature sign-off line was "It's been a pleasure." This image from April 1973 shows Bagli donning the red WBAL News blazer for that evening's broadcast. (Courtesy Bruno Baran.)

Rock with
ROCKIN' ROBIN
WEBB Radio
monday thru saturday
starting at 2:00 p.m.

Cashing in on the popularity of Bobby Day's 1958 record "Rockin' Robin" was deejay Fred Robinson, who used the moniker "Rockin' Robin" on the air. Arriving in 1962, Robinson spent five years with WEBB, which was competing with WWIN and WSID for African American listeners. (Courtesy National Capital Radio & Television Museum.)

Ron Smith came to WBAL-TV in 1973 as news coanchor. He left the station in 1980, then joined WBAL-AM in 1984 for a long-running talk show, calling himself "the Voice of Reason." Smith died December 19, 2011, at age 70. Sue Simmons arrived at Channel 11 from a station in New Haven, Connecticut, in 1974. Two years later, she was anchoring in Washington on WRC-TV. She spent the remainder of her career (1980–2012) presenting the news on WNBC-TV in New York. (Courtesy WBAL-TV.)

Cal Schumann was the voice (and hand) behind J.P. Puppet, who, with Rhea Feikin, presented the weather weekday evenings on WBAL-TV in the late 1960s and early 1970s. The segment ended each evening with J.P. trying desperately to crack up stone-faced anchorman Rolf Hertsgaard. He seldom succeeded. (Courtesy WBAL-TV.)

The dulcet tones of Ed Graham graced Baltimore radio airwaves from 1956 (WWIN) to 1997 (WITH). In the late 1950s, Graham was this close to being hired by the legendary rock station WABC in New York. Returning home after receiving an offer of employment, he found his Army induction notice waiting in the mail. (Courtesy Ed Graham.)

When Dorothy Brunson purchased the bankrupt WEBB in 1979, she became the first African American woman in America to own a radio station. The seller, by the way, was James Brown, "the Godfather of Soul." Brunson died in 2011 at 72. (Author's collection.)

Bob McAllister came to Channel 13 from WTAR in Norfolk in 1963. Hired to replace the departing Gerry Wheeler ("Lorenzo"), McAllister was a magician, ventriloquist, and juggler. His characters included Thurman; twin clowns Willy Winkie and Billie Blinkie; and Melvin Frump, alias Mike Fury, a superhero in search of Silas Sinister. He went to WNEW New York in 1967, where he hosted Metromedia's syndicated *Wonderarma*. McAllister died at 63 in 1998. (Courtesy Bob Bell.)

Robert Campbell "Jake" Embry was a genuine Renaissance man, accomplishing much in his 93 years. An ad salesman for WBAL from 1935, Embry moved to WITH in 1942. He became co-owner of the Bullets basketball team in 1944, and the Baltimore Colts in 1947. Embry helped in the effort to bring the defunct Dallas NFL team to the city in 1953, and in 1962 became president and part owner of the Clippers hockey club. Embry retired in 1982 after 15 years at the helm of WMAR-FM but remained active in business and community events until his death in 2002. (Courtesy National Capital Radio & Television Museum.)

Versatile and popular, Tom Cole moved from WCBM to WBAL-TV in the early 1960s. There, in addition to hosting two bowling shows, he shared the booth announcing duties with Lary Lewman and Royal Parker. (Courtesy WBAL-TV.)

When WJZ needed to replace meteorologist Jim Smith in 1973, they made the process into an effective promotional campaign. Bob Turk was selected, and while not a meteorologist, he established an instant rapport with the on-air staff. Audiences embraced him as well, sending various "pointers" to the station for Turk to use on the station's low-tech weather maps. (Courtesy Devin Turk.)

Dave Humphrey's authoritative baritone voice made him a natural for radio news. After a long stint at WCBM, Humphrey worked at WLIF until the early 1990s, when he left radio for a position in state government. (Courtesy National Capital Radio & Television Museum.)

Bob Shilling's nickname was "Smoke," although some preferred "Smokey." Shilling ran the WCBM newsroom for years, also spending time at WBAL-AM, and WBFF-TV. He enjoyed covering news from the field, especially fires. Shilling was 75 when he died in 2016. (Courtesy National Capital Radio & Television Museum.)

Bill Lefevre paid his dues during a career that began in the 1940s. His stops included WFBR, WMAR-TV, and WFMM-FM (now WPOC) before becoming a host and programmer for WBFF-TV from it debut in 1971. He was also an instructor at the Broadcasting Institute of Maryland, and was active with The Golden Radio Buffs of Maryland. (Courtesy National Capital Radio & Television Museum.)

From left to right, longtime WLIF morning host Dick Ireland poses with station engineer Dwight Weller (once Jim Wells on WLPL), and young Vern Anderson at the WLIF/WFBR holiday party in 1989. Ireland eventually went to WRBS. Weller passed away from cancer in the 1990s. Anderson, who started on WFBR as a teen, moved into television news in Pennsylvania. (Photograph by the author.)

He was a newsman, booth announcer, kids' show host, actor (*Diner*), and commercial pitchman ("Hey, get off of that furniture. Are you trying to ruin it?"). Royal Parker did just about everything anyone could do during a career that began at WASA-AM in Havre de Grace in the late 1940s. (Photograph by the author.)

WMAR's Chuck Richards may have been the most community-spirited man in local history. Born Charles Richardson in 1913, the Baltimore native served on the boards of a plethora of local nonprofits. As a singer, he performed with Duke Ellington and Fletcher Henderson's bands. Richards worked for WITH and WBAL-AM, and was the groundbreaking host of *Chuck Richards Talent Hunt* on Channel 2 in 1951. (Courtesy National Capital Radio & Television Museum.)

Before he became a fixture at WJZ, Ron Matz spent many years covering local news for WFBR, where he had often kibitzed with morning show host Johnny Walker, portraying the flamboyant Hollywood correspondent Harry Horni. In this undated photograph, Matz (left) accepted an award from then-governor Marvin Mandel. (Courtesy National Capital Radio & Television Museum.)

Rolf Harold Hertsgaard was born in Minneapolis in 1922, and like many in the industry, he caught the "broadcasting bug" at an early age. For more than a decade, he wrote and presented news on WCCO in the Twin Cities, then at age 33 left radio to enter a Lutheran seminary. The National Lutheran Council selected him to head their TV division in New York in 1956, which led to the news anchor position at WBAL-TV two years later. (Courtesy WBAL-TV.)

THE BALTIMORE AFRO-AMERICAN   JULY 17, 1965

THE KING OF ALL DEE-JAYS!

FAT DADDY

COMES TO **WITH**

Tiger Radio

GET W-I-T-H IN
MONDAY THRU FRIDAY
8 P.M. TO MIDNIGHT
SUNDAY MORNINGS
7 TO 10 A.M.

Quick! Turn On
WITH
1·2·3 on your dial!

HE'S GRRREAT!

Paul "Fat Daddy" Johnson moved to WITH in 1965, when the station, branding itself as "Tiger Radio," was giving Top 40 WCAO a run for its money in the local ratings. Johnson occupied the air chair weeknights from 8:00 p.m. to midnight, as well as Sunday mornings. (Courtesy Don Lehnhoff.)

From 1967 to 1988, Jack Bowden established himself as a solid field reporter and anchorman at WMAR-TV. Well-liked by coworkers and competitors alike, Bowden got his start on a Frederick radio station before moving to WBAL-FM, then Channel 2. He returned to WBAL—this time AM—after leaving WMAR, then made one last stop in television, at Washington's Channel 7. Bowden also appeared in a few films, most notably *Forrest Gump* and *Cry-Baby*. (Courtesy National Capital Radio & Television Museum.)

Young Gary Michaels was just a teenager when he joined WLPL-FM in the late 1960s. The station's cramped and austere studio was situated in what had been the projection booth of the old Avalon Theatre on Park Heights Avenue. Dethroning WCAO in the ratings, WLPL later moved to more comfortable digs at 6623 Reisterstown Road. (Courtesy Gary Michaels.)

WBAL-TV reporter Ron Canada was chilling out when this photograph was snapped in April 1973. Canada, who left both the station and the industry shortly thereafter, established himself as an actor, with an impressive list of credits in such films and TV shows as *DC Cab*, *Home Alone 2: Lost in New York*, *The Shield*, *Boston Legal*, *Cheers*, and *Star Trek: The Next Generation*. (Courtesy Bruno Baran.)

"Johnny Walker" (James Lewis Embrey) joined WFBR in 1974, taking over for the popular but temperamental Pete "the Flying Dutchman" Berry. Walker did nothing but immediately establish himself as one of the most creative local broadcasters of all time. He was actually the station's second choice to take over mornings. Don Imus was first approached but was too expensive. This 1979 photograph of Walker addressing a Jaycees event was taken at Charles Center. (Courtesy National Capital Radio & Television Museum.)

A native of St. Louis, Al Sanders was born Albert Gay in 1941. After a few years in local radio, Sanders joined WJZ in 1972. After the failed teaming of Oprah Winfrey with longtime news anchor Jerry Turner, Sanders got the nod. Their rapport and affection for each other was more than evident to viewers, and WJZ vaulted to the top of the local TV news ratings. The recipient of two local Emmy awards, Al Sanders was just 54 when he died on May 5, 1995. (Courtesy MARMIA.)

Miss Spiderweb is revealed! WMAR technician John Ziemann portrayed the nemesis of Stu Kerr's Professor Kool during the entire run of the show, from 1967 to 1978. Ziemann has been associated with the Baltimore Colts/Ravens band since 1962. (Courtesy John Ziemann.)

Charley Eckman, "the Coach," could be loud and brash. But he was also a popular sportscaster for WFBR and WCBM and an effective pitchman for Jimmy Wu's New China Inn, among others. With a background as a basketball referee and coach, Eckman moved into broadcasting in 1961, developing the catchphrases "Call a cab" and "It's a very simple game," when being dismissive. (Courtesy National Capital Radio & Television Museum.)

One of the most successful productions in the history of Maryland Public Television, *Wall $treet Week* debuted in 1970 and ran nationally for 32 years. Louis Rukeyser, shown here in an undated photograph, had been a political and foreign correspondent for the *Sun*, before going to ABC-TV as an economics correspondent and commentator. He died in 2006. (Courtesy Fran Minakowski, MPT.)

Eddie Fenton, shown in this undated image, enjoyed an amazing career at WCBM. From high school sports reporter in 1933, to senior political correspondent in Annapolis, Fenton spent 47 years reporting for WCBM, in an industry not known for its longevity. Retiring in 1980, Eddie Fenton, who never drove an automobile, died eight years later at the age of 70. (Courtesy National Capital Radio & Television Museum.)

Rarely seen or celebrated are those who toil behind the scenes. This image of WBAL-TV photojournalist John Davis is presented to represent all the ones who made/make those on the air look and sound good. The photograph is undated. (Courtesy WBAL-TV.)

In 1979, when WFBR obtained the rights to carry Baltimore Orioles games from WBAL-AM, Tom Marr was assigned to join longtime play-by-play announcers Chuck Thompson and Bill O'Donnell in the broadcast booth. Marr also became a weekend sports anchor for WMAR-TV and, ultimately, a popular talk show host at WCBM, joining that station in 1988. Tom Marr suffered a stroke and died July 7, 2016, at 73. (Courtesy National Capital Radio & Television Museum.)

On a warm summer afternoon in June 2001, from left to right, local TV legends Lary Lewman, Rolf Hertsgaard, and Royal Parker gather for lunch and recollections in Pikesville. After leaving WBAL-TV, Lewman ran a hugely successful voiceover business. Hertsgaard owned and operated a Polock Johnny's Polish Sausage franchise between two stints at WITH. Parker made an unsuccessful try for the Maryland House of Delegates and then served on the Baltimore City Liquor License board until 2006. (Photograph by the author.)

As the end of the century neared, the faces of WBAL-TV news included, from left to right, meteorologist Tom Tasselmyer, Virg Jacques, and Donna Hamilton. A Baltimore native, Tasselmyer joined Channel 11 in 1989 after working for stations in Cleveland and Bluefield, West Virginia. Virg Jacques spent seven years at WBAL before moving on to Channels 9 then 5 in Washington. Donna Hamilton joined WBAL in 1995. Prior to that, she cohosted *Evening Magazine* on WJZ. Donna also made appearances in the films *Head of State*, *Line of Fire*, and *Philadelphia*. (Courtesy WBAL-TV.)

Another local boy who made it big was Jack Wells ("I'm at the Copa—Where are you?"). Beginning in the 1940s, Jack spent time at WITH-AM and FM, before getting a popular morning show on WJZ. He went west in the early 1960s, scored as commercial announcer and an actor (*The Doris Day Show*, *The Rifleman*, *The Streets of San Francisco*, *Charlie's Angels*, *The Twilight Zone*, *Night Court*, and others), and lived next door to Charlton Heston. Wells died in 2010 at the age of 86. (Courtesy National Capital Radio & Television Museum.)

CAROL COSTELLO

WBAL11NEWS
BALTIMORE

Carol Costello's career, which began in her native Ohio, paused in Baltimore at WBAL-TV from 1992 to 1995. Since then, she's been with CNN and the Headline News Network. Costello moved to Los Angeles in 2018. (Courtesy WBAL-TV.)

If ever anyone wore many hats, it was Stu Kerr. This former NBC page joined WMAR-TV from WANN-AM Annapolis in 1952. Through 1981, when he was inexplicably fired from WMAR, Kerr was the character the Janitor (also known as the Early Riser), Bozo, Professor Kool, the Conductor on *Caboose*, Mr. Fortune on *Dialing for Dollars*, weatherman, booth announcer, lottery, and *TV Pow* host. (Courtesy John Ziemann.)

Chuck Thompson declined network offers and passed on opportunities to go elsewhere, preferring to stay in Baltimore. His catchphrases like "Go to war, Miss Agnes," and "Ain't the beer cold," were usually saved for special occasions, with the latter serving as title of his 1996 autobiography. (Courtesy National Capital Radio & Television Museum.)

The longtime president and general manager of WFBR was Harry Shriver, shown here in the station's lobby. Many credit WFBR with reviving interest in baseball through their enthusiastic coverage of the Orioles during the 1980s. Morning man Johnny Walker regularly played game highlights from the previous evening set to upbeat music, giving birth to what fans called "Orioles Magic." (Courtesy National Capital Radio & Television Museum.)

Before he became WCBM's "Morning Mayor," Lee Case hosted programs at WFBR and WITH. At the end of his career, he joined WFBR-owned Z-96, WBKZ, which had formerly been WISZ. This photograph is believed to be from the early 1960s, although the venue and event are not known. (Courtesy National Capital Radio & Television Museum.)

A native of State College, Pennsylvania, general assignment reporter Jim Mustard joined WBAL-TV in 1968. Outside of work, two of Jim's interests were motorcycles and railroads. He left Channel 11 in 1990 due to health issues and died in 1994 at the age of 51. (Courtesy WBAL-TV.)

Bailey Goss was host of WMAR's *National Sports Parade* and pitchman for the sponsor's product, National Beer. Born in 1912, Goss and Chuck Thompson were part of the broadcast team for the 1950s Baltimore Colts. He also hosted *Strikes & Spares*, another of WBAL-TVs many duckpin bowling shows. Bailey Goss was only 49 when he died in a 1962 auto accident. (Courtesy John Ziemann.)

A longtime feature on WFBR's midday music program was called *Stump the DJ*, where listeners tried to get the better of host Bob Moke, shown here in an undated photograph. In addition to his air work, Moke became program director for WFBR and WLIF. In 1992, he moved on to DC's WGAY-FM and, eventually, Sirius, where he programmed the 1940s channel until retiring. (Courtesy National Capital Radio & Television Museum.)

Christopher Gaul was a former *Sun* reporter who had two stints in local television; first as investigative reporter for WJZ and then covering medical issues for WBAL. Later, he became writer and managing editor of the *Catholic Review*. A native of Wallasey, England, Gaul died in 2012 at 72. (Courtesy WBAL-TV.)

In early 1968, actor Sebastian Cabot (right) dropped in to the WMAR studios to tape a public service announcement for the March of Dimes. With him was Susan White (later Susan White-Bowden), and John Ziemann (left) with cue card in hand. (Courtesy John Ziemann.)

ROBERT C. ALLEN
MIDDAYS

WCAO
RADIO 60

Robert Alianiello went by many names during his years on radio. In Springfield, Massachusetts, and Philadelphia, he was Bob Allen. In Washington, he went by Russ Wheeler and then Bob Peyton. For a second stint in Philadelphia, he used Tony Edwards. Then in 1969, for WCAO, Alianiello became Robert C. Allen, III. In time, this name stuck, albeit slightly modified to just Robert C. Allen for WLPL, then R.C. Allen for WBAL and Metro Traffic. (Courtesy Tom Conroy.)

Walt Teas ("if you please") was born in 1922 and got his radio start in Dallas in the 1940s. Arriving at WFBR in 1953, Teas was involved with numerous programs and commercial announcements, often working with Flo Ayres. In 1962, he voiced a Muppet for Jim Henson and later provided narrations in various airports, Independence Hall, and the Gettysburg National Battlefield. Teas also recorded voices for the now-defunct Enchanted Forest. (Courtesy National Capital Radio & Television Museum.)

Ron Smith and Sue Simmons did the honors the day Bob Hope dropped in to WBAL-TV. It is reasonable to suggest the subject of golf came up during this interview from the mid-1970s. Simmons was probably accustomed to having celebrities drop by. Her father, jazz bassist John Simmons, worked with the likes of Nat King Cole, Louis Armstrong, and Erroll Garner. (Courtesy WBAL-TV.)

In 2011, Oprah Winfrey told the *Sun*, "Not all my memories of Baltimore are fond ones." WJZ's highly publicized teaming of the young Winfrey with veteran anchorman Jerry Turner was a total flop. But it led to *People Are Talking*, a daily talk show she cohosted with Richard Sher, which resulted in her move to Chicago, fame, and fortune. (Courtesy MARMIA.)

Pete Berry, also known as "the Flying Dutchman," provided WFBR with a major shot in the arm beginning in the early 1970s. Sound effects, crank calls, and all manner of silliness prevailed, including references to Betty, his wife, shown here. "Dutch," as he was called, referred to her as "my semi-lovely bride, Queen Kong." (Courtesy National Capital Radio & Television Museum.)

ALAN CHRISTIAN

radio

WF}R

Talk Radio Thirteen

baltimore

Early television election coverage was definitely low-tech. Here in 1954, WMAR's Dave Stickle stands in front of the vote tally affixed to plain sheets of plywood. Local sponsor Gunther Beer is prominently displayed right there with the vote count. (Courtesy John Ziemann.)

In the 1970s, Alan Christian emerged as one of the first stars of local talk radio. Over the years, he hosted programs on WBAL, WCBM, WFBR, and WITH. (Courtesy National Capital Radio & Television Museum.)

Ted Jaffe was one of Baltimore's first television newscasters, with WAAM-TV. An anchorman before the term even existed, Jaffe's news set at 13 was plain—a reflection of the early days of television—with only a framed picture of the US Capitol Building mounted on the wall behind him. Jaffe went to WCAO when his TV days were over. (Courtesy National Capital Radio & Television Museum.)

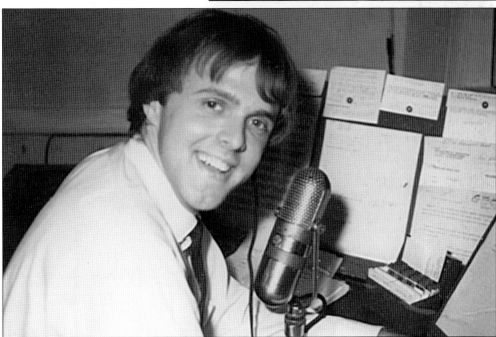

Kerby Confer exploded on the Baltimore radio scene in early 1964. As Kerby Scott, he was king of the evening airwaves on WCAO. Then there were the sock hops, the basketball games, and the television shows, first in Washington and then Baltimore. Investing wisely, he and fellow WCAO jock Paul "The Emperor" Rodgers bought WYRE in Annapolis, the first of more than 50 stations they would own. (Courtesy Don Lehnhoff.)

Local radio newsman Ken Maylath worked for both WFBR and WCBM, where he was news director. He was also a longtime member of the Baltimore Chapter of the National Railway Historical Society, volunteering every week at the Maryland Rail Heritage Library, on the grounds of the Baltimore Streetcar Museum. Maylath died in 2012. (Courtesy National Capital Radio & Television Museum.)

Virginia native Spencer Christian was a news reporter for WWBT-TV in Richmond when he got the call to join WBAL-TV as a weathercaster in 1975. Two years later, he was in New York working for WABC-TV. The exposure resulted in his being hired to do weather nationally on ABC's *Good Morning, America*, a gig he kept from 1986 to 1999. (Courtesy WBAL-TV.)

W·I·T·H Hit Tunes

SURVEYED DAILY—PUBLISHED WEEKLY

TONY DONALD
9:30-NOON

BUDDY DEANE
6-9:30 A.M.

ROZ FORD
MIDNIGHT-6 A.M.

GIL KRIEGEL
NOON-2 P.M.

Featured by the

SOLID • SEVEN

JOEL CHASEMAN
2-6 P.M.

HOT ROD
9 P.M.-MIDNIGHT

$100 WEEKLY
CASH PRIZES

PICK NEXT WEEK'S
"Top Ten Tunes"
(DETAILS INSIDE)

RUSS HALL
6-9 P.M.

Gracing the cover of WITH's weekly music survey in the late 1950s were "the Solid Seven." Clockwise from the top were Buddy Deane, Roz Ford, Hot Rod, Russ Hall, Joel Chaseman, Gil Kriegel, and Tony Donald. WITH offices and studios were at 7 East Lexington Street and, later, 5 Light Street, in the heart of downtown Baltimore. (Author's collection.)

WBAL-TV bowling host Tom Cole found himself at the wrong end of lane number one when this early-1960s photograph was taken. When the station moved to Television Hill, two lanes were installed on the first floor. Later, they were relocated to a former prop storage room on the second floor. (Courtesy WBAL-TV.)

Laurie DeYoung, WPOC's morning host, was voted in to the Country Music DJ Hall of Fame in 2010. Winner of countless awards including the Country Music Association Large Market Personality of the Year in 1994, DeYoung joined WPOC in 1985, having worked for stations in San Diego, Detroit, and elsewhere. (Courtesy Laurie DeYoung.)

Sloane Brown looked to floor director John Ziemann for her cue in preparation for a newscast on WMAR during the 1980s. Since her television days, Sloane has worked in radio for WLIF, as society reporter for the *Sun*, and developed her own line of jewelry and bags. (Courtesy John Ziemann.)

Before he spent 38 years at WJZ, George Baumann was a newscaster for WFBR, as evidenced in this photograph from the 1950s. Baumann, who retired in 1998, was the principal anchorman for WJZ news until 1962, when he was displaced by Jerry Turner. Baumann was 73 when he died in 2003. (Courtesy National Capital Radio & Television Museum.)

Rhea Feikin may be the most well-known woman to appear on Baltimore television. Called "the First Lady of Maryland Public TV," she was a cofounder of Baltimore's Center Stage and has appeared in two films, *Hairspray* and *Cecil B. DeMented*, both directed by friend and fellow Baltimorean John Waters. (Courtesy Fran Minakowski, MPT.)

Bill Jaeger spent 13 years at WFBR and may have conducted the only documented broadcast in history that was received through an EMG machine—albeit unintentionally. In June 1969, a patient in Baltimore's University Hospital was receiving an electromyography when she heard "Windmills of Your Mind," followed by Jaeger introducing newsman Ted Beinart. (Courtesy National Capital Radio & Television Museum.)

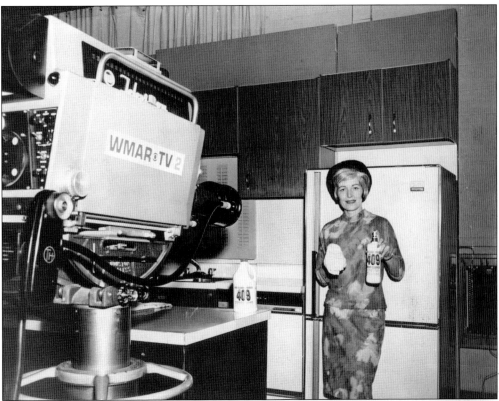

The Woman's Angle was a daily WMAR broadcast. Originally hosted by Polly Drummond and Ann Mar, Sylvia Scott took over in 1959. She also cohosted *Dialing for Dollars*. A native of Cicero, Illinois, she moved to Baltimore in 1943 to take a job at the Glenn L. Martin Company in Middle River. (Courtesy John Ziemann.)

Of all Baltimore broadcasting alumni, Joel Chaseman may be its most financially successful. From humble beginnings at WITH and WAAM, Chaseman rose to top positions for the Post-Newsweek station group, Westinghouse Broadcasting, Chaseman Enterprises International, and King World Productions. (Courtesy National Capital Radio & Television Museum.)

Wiley Edison Daniels Jr. was born in Birmingham, Alabama, in 1929. Following college and military service, he was hired in 1956 at WEBB—first as a deejay, then program director. In 1965, he became a general assignment news reporter at WJZ. In so doing, he was the first African American local television newscaster. Daniels died of a sudden heart attack at 48, on December 8, 1977. (Courtesy MARMIA.)

KAREN FRANCES
radio
WFßR
Talk Radio Thirteen
baltimore

Karen Frances had the challenging job of presenting the news on WFBR during the on-air mayhem known as *The Johnny Walker Show*. Later, she worked at WJHU-FM (now WYPR), and as an independent television producer. (Courtesy National Capital Radio & Television Museum.)

Johnny Walker capitalized on his fame, with a club, commercial endorsements, and even his own book of riddles. Most likely, it is more valuable today as a collector's item than it was when originally published, when it sold for $4 a copy. (Courtesy National Capital Radio & Television Museum.)

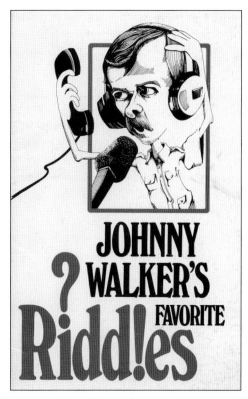

At 18 in 1971, Stan Stovall became the youngest television news anchor in America, working for a station in Phoenix. He had two stints with WBAL-TV, from 1978 to 1983, and then returned in 2003. Before that, he anchored across town on WMAR for 13 years, from 1990. (Courtesy WBAL-TV.)

Born Florence Aaronson in 1923, Flo Ayres was one of the busiest voiceover artists in the region. Working with Walt Teas, Joe Knight, and others, Ayres is credited with thousands of commercials and narrations for local and national clients. Among others, she created the Granny Packer character for Al Packer Ford. Many of Ayres efforts were produced at the now-defunct Flite Three Studios in Baltimore by legendary audio engineer Louis Mills. (Courtesy National Capital Radio & Television Museum.)

Bert and Nancy Claster created *Romper Room* in the early 1950s, with Nancy Claster as host after the person originally chosen backed out at the last minute. Later, "Miss Nancy" turned the local hosting duties over to her daughter, who used the stage name Sally Rogers. (Courtesy John Ziemann.)

Danny Sheelds ("two e's, if you please") worked for WITH in the 1950s and then returned in the 1990s with an hour program on Saturdays. Among other things, Sheelds liked to travel and was especially fond of visiting England. (Courtesy National Capital Radio & Television Museum.)

Receiving her cue from floor director John Ziemann, Beverly Burke worked for both Channels 13 and 2 and has the distinction of being the person who replaced Oprah Winfrey on WJZ's *People Are Talking* after Winfrey moved to Chicago. After her TV years, Burke was heard on WEAA-FM. (Courtesy John Ziemann.)

Danny Reese had radio gigs at WPOC, WITH, and WCAO, after coming to Baltimore in 1973 from a station in York, Pennsylvania. Calling himself "Old Blue Eyes," his death in 2013 at age 61 was attributed to a heart attack. (Courtesy Tom Conroy.)

Samuel Harold Lacy was a journalist and activist for integrated baseball and equal pay. As the first African American member of the Baseball Writers Association of America, Lacy's career began in the 1920s. He appeared on WBAL-TV as a sportscaster, mostly on the weekends, from 1968 to 1976. Sam Lacy wrote his final column, for the *Baltimore Afro-American*, just a few days before his death in 2003, at the age of 99. (Courtesy WBAL-TV.)

Before he became the president of the Mutual Broadcasting System, Bob Hurleigh was a WFBR newsman. In 1941, he inscribed this picture for Eddie "Smokey" Stover, a WFBR engineer. (Courtesy National Capital Radio & Television Museum.)

One of the first local programs to air on WBFF was *Captain Chesapeake*. George Lewis, a one-time WCBM announcer, modeled the captain after kids' show characters he portrayed on stations in Pittsburgh, and Huntington, West Virginia. Lewis hosted the program from 1971 to 1990. (Courtesy Bob Bell.)

The newspaper caption says it all. Johnny Walker, who redefined Baltimore morning radio, died March 1, 2004, at the age of 55. Born James Lewis Embrey in Indiana, Walker was an instant hit from day one on WFBR. After leaving Baltimore, he spent his later years in virtual seclusion at his home in West Virginia. (Courtesy Jay Guyther.)

SUN FILE : 1975

Radio personality dies

Johnny Walker, described as a "creative genius," was host of a morning show on WFBR from 1974 to 1987. (Article, Page 7B)

Thomas Stewart Kerr (1928–1994), looking pensive, sat in the WMAR announce booth awaiting his next cue to speak. Believing his time had passed, Channel 2's management dumped Kerr in 1981. Afterward, he created 54 *Space Corps* for WNUV-TV, became the weathercaster at WJLA Channel 7 in Washington, hosted a weekend radio show on gardening for WCBM, and did other freelance work. A phone interview on WITH six weeks before his death was his final broadcast. (Courtesy John Ziemann.)

About the National Capital Radio & Television Museum

The National Capital Radio & Television Museum is a nonprofit, volunteer organization that has, since 1999, been the central repository for all things radio and television in the Baltimore/Washington region. Located in Bowie, Maryland, the museum has a large number of early radio and television sets on display—some dating back to the 1920s—along with artifacts and memorabilia from area stations.

The idea of a museum grew out of an organization called the Mid-Atlantic Antique Radio Club. With no building or funds, the group collected and borrowed artifacts and displayed them at DC-area libraries, Georgetown University, and a shopping mall in Silver Spring. In time and with the cooperation of the City of Bowie, a location was established in the 1906 Harmel House. The thriving Mid-Atlantic Antique Radio Club now boasts a membership of more than 600.

In recent years, the National Capital Radio & Television Museum became the recipient of a massive collection of local broadcasting files, photographs, equipment, business records, and other ephemera that had been the property of the Golden Radio Buffs of Maryland, now disbanded. Many of the photographs in this publication came from the museum's extensive collection.

The National Capital Radio & Television Museum conducts tours for schools, groups, and other organizations, and they are open to the public free of charge every Friday, Saturday, and Sunday, except holidays. In addition to their files and displays, the museum also offers a 10-week class in how to repair vintage radios, and there is a small gift shop located in the lobby. New members are invited, and the museum welcomes donations and corporate sponsors. They are located at 2609 Mitchellville Road in Bowie. For directions and additional information, call 301-390-1020 or visit ncrtv.org.

DISCOVER THOUSANDS OF LOCAL HISTORY BOOKS
FEATURING MILLIONS OF VINTAGE IMAGES

Arcadia Publishing, the leading local history publisher in the United States, is committed to making history accessible and meaningful through publishing books that celebrate and preserve the heritage of America's people and places.

Find more books like this at
www.arcadiapublishing.com

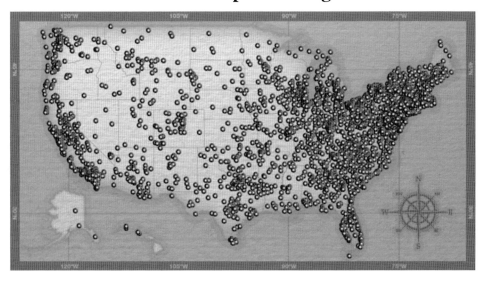

Search for your hometown history, your old stomping grounds, and even your favorite sports team.